A BOY IN BROOKLYN

GROWING UP IN A NORWEGIAN COLONY
IN THE 1940s AND '50s

A BOY IN BROOKLYN

GROWING UP IN A NORWEGIAN COLONY IN THE 1940s AND '50s

ADOLF HANSEN

Cover and interior design by Masha Shubin | AnnoDominiCreative.com
Maps by Jeanne Lewis
Artwork Elements: Knitted Letters, Symbols & Ornaments by Julia Malinovskaya

ISBN-13 978-0-578-36742-2

1 3 5 7 9 10 8 6 4 2

TO

Martha Gundersen Hansen (my mother)

Adolf Hansen, Sr. (my father)

who provided a home where I could develop

TRUST
in
them,
others in the colony,
myself,
and
God

CONTENTS

PREFACE

THIS IS A BOOK ABOUT THE 1940S AND '50S; ABOUT A SPECIFIC place, Brooklyn, New York; about a single group of people, a Norwegian colony; and about a particular person, a boy growing up in this colony.

I was born into this colony and lived there for the first 17 years of my life. And for the past several years, I have been examining my upbringing with considerable care—reviewing documents and photographs, researching unknown or unclear data, and conferring with family, friends, and others who have information and/or insight pertinent to my experience.

My interest in writing this book is threefold: First, to share stories that were, and still are, powerful for me. Second, to describe them in such a way that you, the reader, might connect with them out of your own experience. And third, to invite you to reflect on your own "growing up years," by developing some type of intentional way of responding—as suggested in the "Reader's Reflection" (fifth item in the Appendices).

Of the many individuals who have contributed to the "growing up years" of my life, I especially want to acknowledge and thank those from the colony who assisted me in remembering life during the 1940s and '50s. That process emerged during a series of events: (1) a day and evening gathering of

20 to 30 of us in a suburb of NYC in June of 1988—at a time when I traveled there from my home in Indianapolis; (2) a high school reunion in Brooklyn in June 2005 that included many of these persons; (3) a day-long gathering at a retreat center in New Jersey in October 2015 that once again was comprised of some of the same individuals; and (4) a four-day visit to Brooklyn in May 2018 when I engaged a number of these persons, as well as others, in group settings and individual interviews.

In addition to those from the colony who were present at these events, I want to thank the following individuals with whom I spoke in person or by phone, exchanged electronic communications, received photographs, articles, and editorial suggestions: Madeline Arnott, Rebecca Hansen Arnott, Rick Arnott, Eleanor Pedersen Bensen, Ryan Fifer, Frank and Barbara Govertsen, Ruth Bensen Hansen, Barbara Knudsen Jacobsen, Roy Jacobsen, Rolf Larsen, Michael Shew, and Rigmor Swensen.

I also want to recognize three members of the colony who still live in Brooklyn or Manhattan, and who made pertinent contributions to this book. One is Lois Berseth Hedlund, whom I have known since we were both confirmed at Bethelship Methodist Church in the early 1950s. She wrote the "Historical Development of the Colony" (first item in the Appendices).

The second is Arne Bergman whom I met at the Syttende Mai celebration in Brooklyn on May 17, 2018. He formulated charts that identify the Norwegian establishments on Eighth Avenue between 54th and 60th Streets during the 1950s (third item in the Appendices).

The third is Lars Nilsen, with whom I have communicated a number of times. He has demonstrated significant leadership and entrepreneurial skill in developing and bringing together numerous historical resources that have enabled me to understand more fully the development of the Norwegian colony. One that is of particular significance is his article, "Norway's Presence in New York City" (included in the list of Resources).

In addition, I want to express my appreciation for my editor, Holly Miller, without whom this book would not have come to its intended fruition. She is a published author of numerous articles, a textbook about writing, and several novels. She has taught college courses on writing, as well as served as a coach for writers such as me. In this latter role, she has been an extraordinary mentor, especially since my previous publications have not been in the category of writing stories.

I also want to indicate my indebtedness to Masha Shubin for her creative development and production of the design of the entire book—front and back covers, as well as all the interior elements. She has carried out similar responsibilities for me with three other books published by Inkwater Press. Jeanne Lewis, a graphic artist, assisted her in this process by drawing the maps of the five boroughs in NYC and the neighborhoods in Brooklyn specifically related to the colony (second item in the Appendices).

Finally, I want to share my deep gratitude for Naomi with whom I have been deeply in love, and joyfully married for 62 years. She has carried out numerous activities in support of this project, including the reading of every page—one section at a time—and evaluating its content, grammatical usage, and suitability for publication. In addition, she has taken care of a huge number of household routines and responsibilities that made it possible for me to spend countless hours on the research and writing of this book. And she did this—and a lot more—in incredibly thoughtful ways! Without her extraordinary support, this book would never have been written!

INTRODUCTION

THE PHONE RANG AT 10 A.M. WHILE I WAS EATING BREAKFAST IN THE Brooklyn home of Frank and Barbara, two friends from my early years. Frank quickly picked it up and began talking as he walked out of the kitchen.

After I had eaten a few more bites, Frank returned and handed me the phone, "George would like to speak with you." Frank had talked about George when I had inquired about who chaired the board of the Norwegian Health and Hospital Center—a place I was planning to go that evening to attend their annual banquet. After all, it was the most important day of the year for Norwegians all around the world—"Syttende Mai," the 17th of May—the celebration of Norway's National Day, commemorating the signing of the constitution at Eidsvoll on May 17, 1814.

"It's good to hear from you, George," I said, surprised that he would remember me. "I don't think we've spoken since I graduated from Fort Hamilton High School. And that was more than 50 years ago."

We exchanged a few pleasantries and then George revealed the purpose of his call. He had learned the day before that the keynote speaker for the evening's banquet was ill and couldn't attend this significant event. He had also learned from Frank and Barbara that I was in the process of writing a memoir of my early life in Brooklyn. Was that true? I confirmed that, yes, I had begun to research a book that I hoped my family and a few close friends might find interesting. As I spoke, my thoughts raced ahead. *Surely, he wasn't going to suggest that I . . . .*

"Would you consider being our keynote speaker this evening, and letting us know what you're working on?" asked George. Anticipating my reluctance he quickly added, "I realize this is short notice, but when Frank told me you were coming to Brooklyn to visit locations from your childhood and to interview friends from those years, I knew people would love to hear about the project."

"How much time do I have to think about this?" I asked.

"About a minute!"

In spite of the abbreviated prep, I realized what a great opportunity this would be—to share my intentions for the book, and to gather some colorful anecdotes from persons in attendance at this special banquet. But I needed to tamper down George's expectation. "All I have to offer is a preliminary outline of what I'm planning to write," I cautioned. "I can probably add a few stories that I've jotted down . . . ."

"Sounds great," he answered, obviously anxious to close the deal. "I haven't been in contact with you for decades, but I've heard comments over the years from Frank and Bonnie, and other Norwegian friends. They speak very highly of you. This will be a real treat."

With undeniable trepidation I spent the rest of the day preparing remarks that I hoped would interest the capacity crowd that greeted me several hours later in the banquet hall. The setting was truly celebratory thanks to festive decorations, guests in traditional attire, and a menu that included Scandinavian treats. When George took the podium, he introduced me as a native son with deep roots in Brooklyn's

Norwegian community. The audience was so welcoming that all my doubts disappeared. I truly felt I had returned home.

On the basis of comments from some guests I knew, and numerous others I was meeting for the first time, it became clear that the presentation was well received. Not only were the responses positive, but surprisingly enthusiastic!

Although such a reaction was encouraging, the most important takeaway was the repeated inquiries about getting a copy of the book. What I had been thinking about—writing a book for my family and close friends—might actually be of interest to a wider audience: those who want to learn about experiences of a young boy growing up; those who are interested in Brooklyn in the 1940s and '50s; those who want to learn about a Norwegian colony during that time; as well as others who might enjoy an often humorous, often inspirational story.

That realization led me to broaden the potential audience. As a result, I've expanded my concept, and attempted to include implications of my experiences for others, both within and beyond the colony. I've also delineated more fully my understanding of TRUST, the quality that I believe was of paramount importance to the Norwegian colony of which I was a part—a quality that still permeates all facets of my life.

I've divided the book into four chapters. The first chapter deals with PRE-SCHOOL YEARS (1938-44), when I developed "trust in my parents (and their trust in me)." The second chapter covers GRADE SCHOOL YEARS (1944-50), when I broadened my experience to include "trust in others in the colony (and their trust in me)." The third chapter concentrates on JUNIOR HIGH YEARS (1950-52), when I learned "trust in myself." The fourth chapter takes place in SENIOR HIGH YEARS (1952-55), when I experienced "trust in God (and God's trust in me)."

Following these chapters of the book, I've added five

appendices that pertain to this particular colony. The first sets forth an overview of its historical development. A second provides maps that identify significant locations related to the colony. A third illustrates the preponderance of Norwegian stores in the colony—those along Eighth Avenue, from 54th Street to 60th Street. A fourth identifies the ten sections that comprise each of the chapters. A fifth invites readers to reflect on what they've read, and if they find it desirable, to respond in one or more ways that I suggest.

In the fourth appendix I've identified 10 sections that comprise each chapter. The sequence of the sections is the same in each chapter. This means the narrative that started in Chapter 1 continues sequentially through Chapters 2, 3, and 4. For example, the titles in section seven of each chapter are: 1. *Learning at home*; 2. *Learning in grade school – Public School 169*; 3. *Learning in junior high school – Pershing 220*; 4. *Learning in senior high school – Fort Hamilton 490.*

A concluding part classifies resources I've used in writing the book. The first is a list of pertinent websites. The second is a selection of related Facebook groups, the most useful ones being "Brooklyn Norwegians,"—a private group of 6,100 members, and "Growing Up in Brooklyn"—a private group of 41,500 members. The third is an identification of books and articles I used to broaden and deepen my understanding of the colony.

Throughout this volume I am looking *backward,* since that is the best way to understand my life. At the same time, I am looking *forward,* since that is the best way for me to live my life in a meaningful way!

A BOY IN BROOKLYN

CHAPTER 1

PRE-SCHOOL YEARS

(1938-44)

BORN INTO A COLONY (1)

It occurred at 8:55 a.m. A nurse wearing a white starched hat and uniform came into the waiting room and exclaimed, "You have a boy—8 lbs., 6 ¾ oz." The father beamed with a smile that was wider than any he had ever expressed. He was so elated! He wanted a son more than anything in the world. He already had a daughter.

This joyful day was Wednesday, May 11, 1938. The place was the Norwegian Hospital on Fourth Avenue and 46th Street in Brooklyn, New York—a highly regarded institution in a colony of Norwegian immigrants that had grown rapidly in preceding decades to reach and exceed 62,000 people.

I was the boy who was born that day. I was named Adolf—after my father—though I was often called "Junior" in my early years (an additional name on my birth certificate). The names were pronounced in Norwegian as if they were spelled *Ah-dolf* and *Yun-i-ar* (a three-syllable name, with a long *u* in the first syllable).

After leaving the hospital, I came home to a red-brick, upstairs apartment in a two-story townhouse at 818 56th Street. It had a bedroom for my parents, one for my sister, and another for me; a kitchen with barely enough space for a small table and four chairs, one bathroom for the four of us. The living room led to a porch—open to the sky—with a white wooden railing on three sides, one that I could peer through.

We were only a few buildings from Eighth Avenue, the most significant street for the entire Norwegian colony, since it was replete with stores, restaurants, taverns, travel agents, and offices that catered to the needs of people in the colony.

When my mother was busy in the apartment, she often left me alone on the porch—deeply and firmly believing that being outside was the place to be as much as possible (an understanding of *friluftsliv* that I only began to grasp in the years that followed). First, it was outside in the baby carriage, and then crawling around on the porch floor. I loved being out there, looking through the spindles and seeing all kinds of interesting sights that were often changing, and then changing again.

Since I learned to crawl and even walk by the time I was 11 months old, my parents were concerned that I might try to climb high enough to get to the top of the fence. As a result, my father put up several vertical 2 x 4s, and strung two rows horizontally across them. I wouldn't be able to climb over them—at least not for years to come.

The language spoken in my home was a combination of Norwegian and English, mostly Norwegian when my parents talked with each other, and attempted English when talking to my sister and me. In later years, my friends and I would jokingly call our parents' language "Norlish" or "Engwegian" because it was a mixture of two languages, spoken "Norwenglish." However, we were grateful that our parents wanted us to learn English as our primary language, as well as them trying to learn English on their own. Only when my father dealt with finances, especially counting money, or when he prayed aloud in a heartfelt extemporaneous expression, did he revert to Norwegian.

The atmosphere at home was loving, gentle, accepting, quiet, joyful, and always gracious, always honest, always truthful. Yes, there were disagreements, outbursts of frustration and anger, but they never permeated the atmosphere.

The most profound influence in my life was my mother. She worked at home, spending most of her time with my sister and me; my father worked faithfully outside the home and was only at home for the evening meal and the time thereafter during the week. On Saturdays when he was home, our family often had a time of Bible reading and prayer after breakfast. I was so glad when I was invited to read part of the passage aloud because I could then show I was learning to read. On Sundays our family went to church.

My mother often shared with me, and sometimes with other family members, one of her favorite Bible verses. An oft repeated one was Isaiah 26:4—*Trust in the LORD forever, for in the LORD GOD you have an everlasting rock* (New Revised Standard Version, a translation she used in her later years). This verse and others that dealt with trusting God were among those she cherished most deeply.

My mother's influence led me to have a secure attachment toward her—not an anxious or avoidant attachment (categories I learned as an adult after reading the writings of John Bowlby, Mary Ainsworth, and others). Even before I knew how to express my feelings in words, I experienced them through the warmth that came from my mother.

As I was learning to talk, I spoke almost entirely in English. However, I did learn a few Norwegian expressions that seemed to please my parents and their friends.

Takk, Mange takk, Tusen takk.	"Thanks, many thanks, thank you very much."
Takk for maten.	"Thanks for the food."
Vær så god.	"Here you are," or "You're welcome."
	(literally, "Be so good.")
Vær så snil..	"Please." (literally, "Be so nice.")

I learned many additional expressions in Norwegian later. In that process, I picked up a guttural "r" without realizing it—a sound many people who are not Norwegian can't easily make.

MEETING MY IMMEDIATE FAMILY (2)

According to DNA analyses, my heritage is 91% Norwegian (southern and southwestern) and 9% Swedish. That is not surprising to me since I have met, or am aware of a considerable number of blood relatives of my father and mother. All of them are from locations—as far as I can determine—in southern and southwestern Norway.

My immediate Norwegian-American family begins with my mother and father, immigrants from Norway. My father's name was Adolf Hansen, Sr., born to Reinhart and Gjertine Nilsen Hansen (whom I never met), in Flekkefjord, Norway, on April 1, 1906. Their joint tombstone in Kristiansand reads: *På Jensyn I Himmelen,* or, *See You in Heaven.* My father was baptized on June 3, 1906, in the *Methodistkirke* (Methodist Church) in Flekkefjord. He was formally educated through grade school, but he never attended high school. He went to work to help support his mother and his siblings, since his father—my grandfather—had died.

My father emigrated from Norway on a ship, arriving at Ellis Island in New York City on May 18, 1923, at the age of 17, with his personal belongings packed in two suitcases. He spoke almost no English. He was greeted by a few friends he had met in Norway. They found him a place to stay, provided food on a temporary basis, brought him to their church where services were in Norwegian, and helped him find a job in the construction industry. This was a common pattern for young men coming to the United States from Norway. He became a U.S. citizen on September 24, 1929, at the age of 23. He died in New Fairfield, Connecticut, on December 7, 1980, at the age of 74, when I was 42 years old.

My mother's name was Martha Gundersen Hansen, born to Martin and Amanda Knudsen Gundersen (whom I never met), in Arendal, Norway on June 17, 1898. She was baptized September 4 in the *Methodistkirke* (Methodist Church) in Arendal. She was formally educated only through grade school. She spent time helping her mother care for her seven siblings. She occasionally worked as a nanny and/or a housekeeper.

My mother emigrated from Norway, arriving at Ellis Island in New York City on July 15, 1925, at the age of 27, with only her personal belongings. She spoke English in a limited manner. Like my father, whom she had not met in Norway, she was greeted by friends she had met in Norway. They found her a place to stay, provided food on a temporary basis, brought her to the same church my father was attending, and assisted her in locating homes where she could care for children as well as carry out housekeeping and cooking duties. This was a common pattern for single women coming to the United States from Norway. She became a U.S. citizen on May 18, 1943, at the age of 45. She entered the Norwegian Christian Home and Health Center in Brooklyn, New York, on June 3, 1981—six months after my father died—and lived there for 10 years. She died on

December 29, 1991, at the age of 93—when I was 53 years old—and was buried next to my father in New Fairfield, Connecticut.

My mother met my father at Carroll Street Methodist Episcopal Church in Brooklyn at a time when he was married to my mother's sister, Nancy Gundersen, who had emigrated from Norway on October 29, 1924. However, she died from pneumonia three years after they were married. They had no children. Subsequently, my father and mother married on April 17, 1934. It's interesting that my father's informal greeting to others when the three of them were together—Nancy on one arm and my mother on the other—was to introduce them as "my first wife," and then, "my second wife." Though he didn't really mean this, that's the way it turned out. Yes, interesting!

My sister's name was Elsie June, born on February 5, 1935, at the Norwegian Lutheran Hospital in Brooklyn located at that time on Fourth Avenue and 46th Street—three years before I was born. She started school early at the age of 5 (since her birthday was in February), enrolling at Public School 105 (in the center of the colony). After we moved in 1944, she transferred to PS 169 (at the edge of the colony)—the year I entered first grade at the same school. She continued at that school through eighth grade (an option for girls, but not for boys who had to leave after sixth grade). She then enrolled at Bay Ridge High School (for girls only) in 1948 at age 13, where she studied Norwegian as one of her academic subjects.

In the summer of 1950, when Elsie was 15, and I was 12, we moved to a third apartment. And in the fall of that year, she left home to attend Hillcrest Lutheran Academy in Fergus Falls, Minnesota, a private high school that had a number of students from the Norwegian colony in Brooklyn, for her last two years. Overall, it was not a good experience for her. She was simply too young to handle all the freedom she was given.

I entered Pershing Junior High at the time she left, and Fort Hamilton High when she returned. We only lived together in this third apartment for one year, after which she moved out to marry a student from her high school *alma mater.* We never developed a significant relationship.

Years after I left Brooklyn, I connected with Elsie in more mature ways. One was my awareness of her successful professional career, serving in her last position as the Controller of a large NYC architectural firm. As a woman in a world where her peers in other corporations were men—often with MBA degrees—she was appropriately proud that she had attained a level far beyond her expectations, since she had only taken two accounting courses at the collegiate level, and had never received an undergraduate degree. I was proud of her too!

Elsie and her husband moved from NYC to Arendal, Norway, for their retirement years. Some years later, I made a special trip to visit her in a hospital in Arendal, since she was ill, and not expected to live much longer. I spent several days with her, but was not able to engage in much meaningful communication. She died on December 22, 1996, in that same hospital room a few days after I returned to the U.S. She was 61 years old; I was 58.

I tried my best to connect with her during the days I was with her, but there was little interaction that I could understand. I told her I loved her—over and over again—but I'm not sure what she was able to comprehend. Prior to leaving for the airport, I held her hand, prayed with her, kissed her on the forehead, and said goodbye. It was a very sad day.

This is the extent of my immediate Norwegian-American family.

CONNECTING WITH FRIENDS BEYOND MY IMMEDIATE FAMILY (3)

During my pre-school years, most of my friends were

Norwegian-American (simply called *Norwegian*). They were children—my own age and older—as well as parents, aunts, uncles, and cousins. This was not unusual. Such intergenerational relationships permeated the entire colony.

In the Bay Ridge section of Brooklyn where I grew up—currently called Sunset Park—other ethnic groups functioned in similar ways to Norwegian-Americans. A predominant one was Italian-American (simply called *Italian*). This was the ethnic identity of the man who owned the building where we initially lived. His apartment was on the first floor; ours was on the second. He was such a friendly man, especially fond of children like my sister and me. He exemplified many of the same behaviors as the Norwegian adults I was meeting, not only in my immediate neighborhood, but also in the church my family attended—those we called our church family.

Sometimes the Norwegian adults I met became close to me, functioning as if they were an actual part of my family. One was Mrs. Frøysa. She lived with her husband next door to us, not in a literal sense, because they really lived *next porch* to us. Only a railing—about three feet high—separated our two upstairs apartments. The spindles allowed me to look into their porch, just like the spindles on the other side of the porch, as well as the front, that let me look down to the street.

What I loved most was when Mrs. Frøysa would bend down and talk with me through the spindles of the railing. She usually did this when she was on the porch and saw me coming toward the railing. I liked this face-to-face contact, especially when she asked if I wanted a treat. I didn't know what it would be, but I smiled and nodded. And it was always something sweet—candy, a cookie, or ice cream in a cup, or on a stick. It tasted so good—every time!

One day she conferred with my mother and—as far as I could figure out what was going on—asked if she would be willing to lift me over the railing for a brief visit. I didn't understand what was taking place, but my mother turned to me and asked, "Would you like me to lift you up and hand you over the railing to Mrs. Frøysa?" I don't think I said any words; I just smiled, and raised my hands for my mother to pick me up. She did. Mrs. Frøysa reached out to me with outstretched arms, held me, and hugged me, just like my mother would.

Mrs. Froeysa became like another mother to me in the six years I lived *next porch* to her. And so did many other mothers and fathers who lived in our Norwegian colony, as my mother and father became parental figures to their children.

I visited a number of other Norwegian homes—usually an apartment, though sometimes a house—with my sister before she started school, but most often after I was home alone. Telling stories and eating Norwegian goodies were prevalent, together with playing planned and impromptu games. It was usually a joyful time, filled with exuberant laughter and fun! And what was so delightful, we could simply walk to most of the homes we visited!

I became acquainted with many other children and their families, both in my immediate neighborhood, and in places that necessitated a longer walk—often where our *church family* lived. These experiences made me feel like I had an especially large family, when in reality I only had one sister who was more than three years older, who understandably wanted to play with friends her own age.

One incident that enabled parents of other children to learn about me was an advertisement in the Brooklyn Section of the Sunday News, dated January 19, 1940—when I was 1 ½ years old, featuring a portrait of me, taken by HERBERT, *Brooklyn's Well-Known Child Photographer,* located at 23 Flatbush Avenue. It read: *Extra Special for This Week—1 large 8 x 10 portrait, complete in folder $1.* Or, *6 photographs, 5 x 7, in book form $5.*

And a notation at the bottom: *Please present advertisement before February 3.* (I still have a copy of the ad.)

My parents were so proud of the various poses in the photographs, that they purchased numerous copies for themselves and other family members, including one 11 x 17 still hanging on my bedroom wall (photo also on back cover). When a number of persons in the Norwegian community saw the ad, or heard about it from my mother or my father, they spoke with my parents, and subsequently with me as occasions arose.

ATTENDING AN IMMIGRANT CHURCH (4)

I have no recollection of that first Sunday morning in church, but my mother described the nursery room to me—over and over again—as I grew up. It was crowded. Most babies were fussing, some even crying, but volunteers who cared for the infants were joyful, gentle, and kind. They seemed to exemplify the same spirit Jesus expressed when people brought children to him.

My mother was so proud that, at the age of 40, she had borne a healthy son in a land that was foreign to her, a land where her mother and father and most of her family didn't live. She also found deep satisfaction in the love shown to her by her husband, her family (most of whom were thousands of miles away), her many friends at church, and—yes—especially God!

On that Sunday morning, I started my venture of becoming a disciple of Jesus Christ. It was followed by my weekly visits to that same nursery, my subsequent baptism on October 2, 1938, when I was 4 months old. In the years that followed I listened to Bible stories, sang songs, and talked to God in prayer—at home as well as at church.

The name of that church was Bethelship Norwegian Methodist Church, located on the corner of Fourth Avenue and 56th

Street, the same street where I lived, though five long blocks away. I say *long* because the distance between avenues in this section of Brooklyn was twice as long as the distance between streets.

The first part of the name of the church was a combination of two Hebrew words *beth* (house) and *El* (God, a shortened form of *Elohim*). Joined together, this part of the name became *Bethel* (House of God). The second part was the word *ship*, taken from the original location of the church on the deck of a barge in the New York City harbor. Thus, the first word in the name of the church was *Bethelship*.

The original location was established by Norwegian lay people residing near the harbor who were concerned that the options for Norwegian seamen during evenings and weekends were often limited to frequenting taverns or shacking-up with prostitutes. To provide an alternative option, one that included a way to find and develop a meaningful relationship with Jesus Christ, they purchased an old barge in 1845, one tied up to a pier that no one seemed to want. Since a number of the laymen were employed in construction, they pooled their limited resources, built a large open room for preaching and teaching, as well as for fellowship with other Norwegians residing in the colony.

To foster a gracious environment, and to serve food—especially Norwegian delicacies—the women were also a very important part in providing an atmosphere of meaningful fellowship, though they had to be cautious relating to men who had not spent much time with women since leaving ports in Norway and other stopovers.

Members of the congregation who were involved in the ministry taking place on the barge decided, for a variety of reasons, to join with others and move to a different location—*on land*—and established the Carroll Street Methodist Church in 1878. Lay people from that congregation purchased a building in 1934 that became Bethelship Norwegian Methodist Church. It remains at that location today, though its name was changed to Bethelship Norwegian United Methodist Church in 1968. That is the name on the sign outside the church today, and the identity that is given to the building. However, Norwegians no longer attend the church (except for occasional visitors). The largest group to worship there are the Gujaratis from India, though others from Central America also attend. At the present time there is one worship service and multiple classes in English on Sunday morning. The Fourth Avenue United Methodist Church gathers on Sunday afternoon for a service in Spanish. In addition, the Ministerio Bethel Internacional meets there on Sunday evening for a service in Spanish. It has become a multi-cultural church.

A strong impression that stays with me to the present day is the visual imagery of the sanctuary, particularly the artwork on the front chancel area wall. Upon entering the church or sitting in any pew in the room, a visitor encounters a depiction of Jesus, after his resurrection, walking with two men. One man was called Cleopas in the Gospel according to Luke; the other disciple is not identified by name. Its impact on me was not only the imagery of a person walking with Jesus, but of me walking with Jesus.

The other impression came from the imagery painted on the large wall on the left side of the room, high enough to contain two separate images. The bottom one is the 19th century depiction of the barge tied up to the pier, with the room built on it—the one originally called *Bethelship.* Then, on the upper part of the wall is a rendition of Jesus reaching out to Peter on the Sea of Galilee when Peter thought he was drowning—a reminder of a first century event, as well as the water being a central place for the seamen and others worshipping in the sanctuary. It also had an impact on me—and still does—of Jesus reaching out to others in dire circumstances.

I looked at the sanctuary imagery on most Sundays during the school year for more than ten years. It became part of my identification with Jesus that has never left me!

GETTING ACQUAINTED WITH A NEIGHBORHOOD (5)

The first apartment where I lived was on a one-way street with parking available, though not always taken, on both sides—a typical layout for most of the streets, though not avenues, in Bay Ridge in the 1940s and '50s. The surface was a smooth blacktop on the streets where I played, with round sewer covers in the center every 100 to 200 feet, and rectangular drains along the curb. Chalk was often used to write messages, draw game markers (bases for stickball, goalie boxes at the ends of our so-called hockey courts, and several others). Interspersed along the sides of the street were *johnny pumps* (fire hydrants) that residents used during hot, humid summer months when police, or others (sometimes without permission), opened them for children to play in the rushing water.

Neighborhoods like mine were delightful places to live. There was so much to see, hear, and touch. I was in the midst of it all after I came home from the hospital. I was captivated by sensory intrigue and excitement, whether I looked through a window or went outside—on the porch or down on the street. And this environment was not unique to those who were a part of the colony into which I was born. It was the setting for all of us who were living in Brooklyn during those years.

I saw so many interesting things from my perch on the porch: the long row of two-story townhouses to my right, with people often on the porches during warm weather; the four-story apartment building to my left, set back from the sidewalk, providing a view of incredible activity on Eighth Avenue at all hours. And interesting sights on 56th Street itself—right below where I lived.

During these early years I began to hear sounds that I initially didn't understand very well, but learned more fully during the years that followed. Some of them were typical urban sounds such as cars, horns, sirens, and a variety of voices—moms calling children, youth interacting with each other in street games, neighbors connecting with each other—some talking, some laughing, some yelling, some singing or playing instruments.

But that was not all! There were sounds such as trolley cars moving along metal tracks that screeched with noise coming from metal rubbing against metal—eerily heard all day long—especially when I lived close to the tracks on Eighth Avenue the first few years of my life. And in the midst of those trolley sounds was the ringing of a bell each time a passenger wanted to get off.

I also heard incessant foghorns from the harbor, awakening me from sleep on heavily overcast days; numerous shrill sounds from all types of whistles; church bells, sometimes every 15 minutes; fire crackers punctuating the air, even on days and nights not related to a holiday; underground subways and elevated trains creating all sorts of noises while running through the neighborhood.

I can still recall the sounds of the seltzer fountain in the candy store; coal running down chutes directly from a delivery truck or a wheelbarrow in narrow alleys; *clop, clop, clop, clop,* the sounds from the horse-drawn wagons coming down the street to deliver milk and other dairy products, vegetables, or fish. Vivid in my memory is the noise from huge steel-surfaced wheels of carts pushed by the man who called out to neighbors as he collected clothes, metals of any sort, or simply newspapers, cardboard, or old rags. And then there was the rambling of garbage trucks and sanitation department trucks hosing down streets with water; roller skating in the streets more than the sidewalks; and trucks offering services such as knife and scissor sharpening, or amusement rides for children like the whip, sky swing, or carousel.

I played outside as much as possible, usually on the sidewalk between our apartment and Eighth Avenue. It was a safe place to be. At first, when I was learning to walk, my mother went with me; but when I could walk by myself, she sat on the stoop and watched me, having given me instructions to stay on the sidewalk, and not go any farther than we could see each other. She commended me every time I returned to her after I stayed within those boundaries. She also told me that one day I would be able to play outside by myself. I really liked that and was very careful to stay within those boundaries.

That way of playing outside was fine with me for additional months, since I could go all the way to Eighth Avenue where there was so much to experience. And, then one day, my mother asked me what I thought of the idea of her being outside on the porch rather than on the stoop. I told her I liked that as long as I could still see her. She said, "Ok, let's try it, and see how that will work." My attachment was still secure, though it was being tested.

After a few times playing outside by myself, my mother asked if I liked playing without her sitting on the stoop. I smiled and told her it was fine; I even liked it. I played a few more times that way—supervision from a distance. And, not long after, she said, "If I have to go inside for something, will you be ok if you can't see me for a little while?" I think she sensed that I wasn't sure. She said, "Tell me when you think that might be ok."

My father, whom I often called *Papa,* and my mother, whom I often called *Mama,* had recently bought me a red tricycle. I loved it. I could ride it fast (as I understood the word at that time), up and down the sidewalk—all by myself! I was so proud, and felt such a new sense of independence! Papa, as well as Mama, affirmed this and said it was ok to ride the tricycle outside by myself. I really liked that! Soon thereafter I told Mama she didn't need to stay on the porch. She agreed, though indicated she might come outside to see how I was doing. She did that once or twice—maybe a lot more than that—and I enjoyed my freedom so much that I forgot to look up on the porch to see if Mama was there.

Then, one day, I stared at the fire alarm box on the corner, close to the curb—bright red, just like my tricycle—and thought it would be a lot of fun if the bright red fire engine could come, sounding its siren. I kept thinking about it—over and over again. I didn't know there were words near the very top that read: "To send FIRE ALARM—Lift Guard and Pull Handle—FDNY." Of course, I didn't see, and couldn't read, any of the words. I was only 3—possibly 4—at the time.

I parked my tricycle against the large, circular column, stood up on top of its red, metal seat and reached as high as I could for the big handle. I realized I couldn't quite reach it. Then a woman—a total stranger—came up to me and asked: "What are you trying to do?"

"Would you help me? I want to see the fire engine, and hear the siren. I can't reach the handle," I answered.

"You mustn't do that," she responded in a loud, angry voice. "Pulling the handle is only used when there is a real fire!" Before I could say anything further, she put her hands on my waist and firmly lifted me down. And then she asked, "Where is your mother?"

I don't want my mother to find out, I thought. I simply got on my tricycle and quickly found myself peddling down 56th Street, heading home. I kept thinking: *I didn't go in the street—I didn't go past the corner—I stayed in the boundaries.* As I was slowing down, I looked up at the porch. My mother wasn't there. I was so glad!

Did I tell my mother? No. I was too afraid of what the consequences might be. I just sat on the steps and was glad the fire engine hadn't come that day.

EXPERIENCING ANOTHER NORWEGIAN COLONY (6)

Brooklyn was not the only location for a Norwegian-American colony. Others were in metropolitan NYC, and in larger numbers in Minnesota, North and South Dakota, and Wisconsin. In addition to these colonies, were gatherings of much smaller numbers in places such as Candlewood Lake in southwestern Connecticut—approximately 80 miles from the Brooklyn colony.

I am not sure how that location was chosen, but I am certain of what developed there. My mother and father were among the first persons who bought property in those hills less than two miles from the northwest section of Candlewood Lake known as Squantz Pond State Park. That property was reached by an oiled road covered lightly with sand. It had a turn-off on to a dirt road, that years later became known as Rocky Hill Road.

The entire road from the lake to the properties was uphill, with an early part so steep that cars with a stick shift (most of them in the late 1930s and early '40s) had to come to a stop before starting up the hill in order to shift into first gear. Arriving at the top, motorists had a magnificent view of the water, lined with trees and shrubs along the shore. Very few buildings were visible, since most of the land was integral to the state park. It reminded these Norwegians of their home country, and became the primary reason for a family to buy property and build a *hytte* (cabin) in the woods.

My father drove a 1939, four-door, black Chevrolet that he bought as a used car in the early 1940s, and kept it running in excellent condition until 1955. The headlights were seated on top of the front fenders, and the tail lights attached separately from the body; the handles of the doors were next to each other, enabling the doors to open in opposite directions; and the five pedals on the floor were called starter, accelerator, brake, gearshift clutch, and headlight adjuster.

That uphill climb from the lake continued to a dirt road on the right side. After driving an additional quarter mile, the road leveled off and simply became a walking path into the woods. A brook with seasonally changing levels of water ran along the last section of the dirt road, with an attractive open area on a hilltop on the other side of the brook. A family by the name of Hansen—not a relative of ours—purchased a few acres of land there in the mid-1930s, with a plan to build a road across the brook, with large pipes underneath it to carry the water from the brook. They sold four lots to other Norwegian-American families—Olsen, Jacobsen, Pedersen, and Wagenes—and kept one for themselves. In 1937, a year before I was born, my parents purchased a steep wooded hillside at the end of the road. The Bensen family bought the lot next to them. In addition, the two lots next to them had already been purchased by two German immigrant families, Schirrmeister and Nussle, who became dear friends with those in this emerging Norwegian colony.

Most of these Norwegian families knew each other because they were part of Bethelship Norwegian Methodist Church in Brooklyn. Other Norwegian families from Brooklyn also purchased lots on the two roads leading up from the lake: Strand,

Andersen, Trost, Gulbrandsen, Hals, and Soyland (Carl, the editor-in-chief of the Nordisk Tidende, a Norwegian language newspaper in Brooklyn). Each of the families built their own *hytte*, most of which became houses that were eventually winterized.

The cultural context that motivated many Norwegian immigrants was the practice in Norway of families having an urban home close to where they were employed, and also to have a *hytte* in the countryside, usually located in scenic hillsides, often wooded and near a fjord, a lake, or other stream of water. And that is precisely what these wooded locations in close proximity to Candlewood Lake offered these families. It was a reminder of their fatherland or motherland. Furthermore, it was a deep emotional connection for them, and to some extent their families, that enabled them to experience *Norway* here in the U.S. Every time my parents went to our *hytte*, they went to Norway emotionally. For them it was a state of mind, a state of soul, a state of being. I learned the depth of this sentiment as an adult. I wish I would have learned more of what they were experiencing when I was a child!

Engaging in the life of this colony in Connecticut enabled me to understand my Norwegian heritage more fully: why they wanted to go there on weekends as often as possible; why my father went there at every opportunity that became available, even when he had to go alone; and why we lived there every summer during the first 12 years of my life.

My parents never owned a house in Brooklyn. They now owned property on which to build a house. Soon after I was born, they began to take down dozens of trees by axe and lengthy hand saws pulled back and forth by two men. During the following summer, they tried to explain (though I didn't understand most of what they told me), where the driveway would begin—at the place where the dirt road ended—and move uphill alongside a lengthy wall of stones, stacked by the former owner of the property years earlier.

One day early that summer—when I had learned to walk—my parents, with my sister (5 years old at the time), and I sauntered up the steep path next to the stone wall until it came to an end. And then, after moving a short distance to the right, my father picked me up, and the four of us gazed over the hillside to the dirt road—hundreds of feet away. It was a delightful view, though I could only see it and feel it, not actually understand it.

The following summer, when I was 3 years old, I began to crawl over and under branches teeming with intriguing shapes of the leaves, the names of which came later—oak, maple, and tulip. Sometimes my mother didn't know where I was, but that didn't concern her. She was busy working among the branches. She listened only occasionally to make sure I wasn't calling out to her. She also listened to determine whether I was humming. If she could hear me, she would know I was ok. She let me go wherever I wanted to go. This approach gave me such a sense of freedom!

I'm not sure why I hummed, but I did seem to enjoy it. Was it a sign of concentration? An imitation of a bee, or other insect? A preverbal expression? A way to combine non-verbal awareness of two languages spoken in my family? A recollection or a composition of a musical tune? Was it a way of responding to my environment, particularly since I didn't have books to look at, or anyone to read stories to me? Was it a way of indicating I was interested in something? Was it an expression of my feeling secure and content? Or, was it some combination of these possibilities? I don't know, but I liked the feeling it produced!

In the next few years, my father, who oversaw the ongoing development of the property, had a bulldozer come and remove additional trees, put in a dirt driveway, and level an area where a house could be built. With the help of a neighbor, and a few other men from the colony in Brooklyn, they erected a large rectangular room—approximately 20 x 30 feet—with black tarpaper on the outside held in place by random slats of wood. A shingled roof, wooden floors, two doors, several windows, 2 x 8s for the ceiling, and 2 x 4s dividing the interior space, completed the first phase of our own house.

During this time, I watched and helped my father on occasion, but most of the time I played with other children during the day. Sometimes my mother would join with us in a particular activity; she was a lot of fun. Children throughout our summer colony loved her playfulness. They even gave her a special name. A young girl couldn't pronounce *Boffie,* the nickname adults had given my mother. Instead of calling her *Tante Boffie,* the girl called her *Tante Bodie* (pronounced as it was spelled *Boodie*). However, my mother spelled it with one *o* rather than two. She, therefore, became known as *Tante Bodie*, a name that adults as well as children used throughout her entire life.

One evening, after we had finished eating supper, my mother asked me to see if some of the other children wanted to join us for a walk down to the main road—a distance of at least a quarter of a mile. It didn't take long for them to show up, having gotten permission to go. Off we went as the sun was setting. Who would the children have chosen as their favorite adult for such a walk? Yes, my mother! All of us loved these times, particularly when we could see lightning bugs (fireflies) in all directions. When we would hear a noise in the woods, my mother would turn on her flashlight and point it in the direction of the noise we heard. If we didn't see an animal, we would just be quiet, and listen very intently for a short time. If we didn't hear anything further, we would keep walking.

That evening, when we arrived back at our driveway, it was

dark, except for the beautiful moonlight illuminating our way. Then, all of a sudden, we heard a rustling in the woods—30 to 40 feet in front of us! We immediately stopped and listened. The sound continued, and then we saw an animal show up at the edge of the driveway, momentarily pause, and then walk slowly across it. I'm sure everyone was really scared! I certainly was, especially when I saw the animal was black and had a white stripe on its back that led to a bushy tail. I was sure it was a skunk; I had seen one before. We all remained motionless, not wanting to scare it into sending a horribly smelling spray on us. And before we could even begin to grasp what was happening, a second smaller one followed, then a third, and finally a fourth following close behind. No one said a word. Mother turned to us with a finger on her lips, and a very quiet *shh* coming from her mouth. No one moved a muscle, as we listened to the rustling continue through the woods.

When we got to the top of the driveway, we talked and laughed, and had fun thinking of what could have happened. We also heard my mother say, "Remember not to frighten animals of any kind when you see them in the woods or on the road. They won't hurt you, or even bother you, if you don't scare them." My friends and I followed what she told us, and had many good times watching, and even playing with some of the animals we met on the road, or in the woods.

My friends and I went for walks during the day, sometimes led by Elsie, who was the oldest member of our group. We sometimes stopped by homes of neighbors in the colony. On one such occasion we stopped by to say "hello" to Mrs. Strand—who had no children of her own. Remembering that my mother had told me never to ask for candy, while—at the same time—wanting a piece of her wonderful Norwegian chocolate, I simply asked, "Mrs. Strand, do you like candy?" All I remember was that she grinned, asked us to wait for a minute, and then returned with a piece of chocolate for each of us.

How do I remember that wording—which I thought would follow my mother's instruction, and still get us a piece of chocolate? My mother told me the next day what Mrs. Strand had shared with her; and then she looked at me, smiled, and gave me a hug!

On Sunday mornings, my friends and I would put on our spiffy clothes and head for Mrs. Olsen's house for our Sunday School lesson. She would have us come into her living room where she had a pump organ, with a separate pedal for each foot. We were fascinated by the sounds she produced as each of the pedals were pushed—over and over again—while her hands played the keyboard, and her elderly voice led us in our singing of choruses and hymns. She also shared Bible stories and ways they related to our lives. She was an incredibly gracious lady!

LEARNING AT HOME (7)

I started my formal education in public school in the fall of 1944, when I was 6 years old. I did not attend preschool or kindergarten. As far as I know those options were not available, at least not in the community where I grew up. Prior to that time, my learning took place at home, or through connections with my home: family, neighborhood, church, and others in the colony.

My mother was central to my early learning. My sister was initially at home, but started school in 1940, when I was 2 years old. This left my mother and me in the apartment, or in places where we went together. During those years my mother told me a lot of stories, especially from her childhood in Norway. A favorite involved her going to church in a rowboat. But she didn't read any stories to me because she couldn't read from books written in English. Neither did she help me learn letters, words, and numbers, not because she did not want to, but because she was not able. As a result, we had no books at home other than copies of the Bible, one in English and one in Norwegian. Yes, there were coloring books and crayons, but they were filled with pictures, not words.

One of the impacts of these limited options was the development of my imagination. As I learned from my mother about Norway, she told me stories about the town of Arendal, where she had grown up. She showed me the few photographs she had, but they were mostly poses of family members. I made up additional pictures in my mind to go along with the stories she was telling me.

I also developed my imagination by coming up with images from the stories broadcast on radio stations ABC, CBS, and NBC. (Television had not yet become a widespread reality.) I remember *Henry Aldrich,* the program that started with the call of Henry's name, and his response, *Coming, Mother!* I also recall, *Digby O'Dell, the Friendly Undertaker,* who ended his comments by saying in a deep voice, "I must be shovelin' on!" Also, *Fibber McGee and Molly,* when McGee opened the hall closet and all sorts of bric-a-brac came clattering down, he would say "I gotta get that closet cleaned out one of these days." And dozens of other shows during this Golden Age of Radio.

My mother almost always smiled as she looked at me, as well as other people. As she did this, she spoke with a joyful tone of voice, often with a bit of laughter and a twinkle in her eyes, evoking a joyful response from others. She did this when she was playing a game, especially if I was playing with her, and winning (or her letting me win). We loved to play games like Chinese checkers, pic-up sticks, dice games, card games such as Old Maid—particularly when she ended up as the old maid. We also had a lot of fun making things with cardboard boxes and other packing items, blankets over chairs as well as creative endeavors using paper, pencils, crayons, clay, paste, and so forth.

We not only did things inside (whenever it was raining or bitterly cold), but we went out as much as possible—honoring her commitment to *friluftsliv.* At first, it was using the large and beautiful carriage. Although I don't know how common it was, my mother got the carriage from another mom; and after I was able to sit in a stroller, passed the carriage on to still another mom in the colony who had a new-born child. We went to stores, the laundromat, events in the neighborhood, and homes of other people, including occasional prayer meetings with a small group of Norwegian women at the home of Mrs. Samuelsen—where I was as quiet as a mouse, listening to the women speaking softly and praying reverently.

At home I learned to pray, first at mealtime, where we said the same prayer at every meal—a prayer that virtually every resident in the Norwegian colony spoke in unison. It is a prayer that came from Norway (and translated into English in literal and/or poetic wording):

I Jesu navn gar vi til bords,	In Jesus name we go to the table,
Og spiser, drikke pa ditt ord.	And eat and drink according to his word.
Deg, Gud, til aere, oss till gavn,	To God the honor, us the gain,
Sa far vi mat i Jesu navn.	So we receive food in Jesus' name.
Amen.	Amen.

Other activities that were expressions of faith took place outdoors. A primary one was the annual Sunday School parades that brought together several hundred children, their parents, teachers, and other church workers, to walk together in groups representing individual congregations. Yes, there were baby carriages and strollers, but most children walked with paper sashes across their bodies, with symbols as expressions of faith, and names identifying the churches they represented. Adults carried large cloth banners, either horizontally or lifted high on a pole, at the beginning of a new group.

In addition, there were dignitaries of all types—representing congregations, denominations, and social organizations. Musical groups were interspersed throughout the parade, as were floats and displays. Major avenues such as Eighth Avenue, as well as other streets, were the locations for the marches, and were closed to vehicular traffic. Although this was not a parade limited to Norwegians, a large segment of those marching, or standing along the parade route were, since the predominance of those participating were from churches in the colony.

A key to my learning at home was the secure attachment to my mother. The coregulation of emotions between the two of us—my internalizing hers, yet becoming weaned off her emotional dependence—helped me to develop my own inner resources. It was based on imitation at first, then freedom to act on my own. My mother was a secure base for me, and allowed me to go out and explore the world. I am deeply grateful for all I learned from her in those preschool years.

ENGAGING IN ACTIVITIES BEYOND HOME (8)

I began observing outside activities from the upstairs porch soon after I was born. There was so much to see, and it was so interesting—though I didn't understand a lot of what I was seeing. I kept observing from a carriage and a stroller; then walking, pulling a wagon, riding a tricycle, climbing, roller skating, and looking through the window of a trolley, or the passenger seat in the car (with no restraint or car seat of any kind). I loved to see the world outside!

I enjoyed going places with my mother, especially trips on Eighth Avenue, a major thoroughfare those of us in the colony called *Lapskaus Boulevard* (the name of a Norwegian stew). Our most common ventures were to stores along that avenue, where my mother could leave me outside, strapped in the carriage or stroller. I liked looking in the windows of the stores, often not knowing what I was seeing, but liking what I saw—especially at the fish market.

I also liked our trips to parks, particularly the walk on Eighth Avenue to Leiv Eriksson Square, an area with boundaries that have fluctuated over the years (though primarily 65th to 66th Street). It was established in 1925, named after the explorer who first sailed to the North American continent, and dedicated as a playground primarily for mothers and their children by NYC Mayor Fiorello LaGuardia on Columbus Day in 1934. Then, in 1939—when I was 1 year old—a bronze plaque (22 x 30 inches) was added, showing the figure of a man standing at the prow of a Viking ship with an inscription that read *"Leiv Eriksson Discovered America in the Year 1,000."* Following years of discussion regarding the name, it eventually became known as Leif Erickson Park.

April – July 1939 (when I was one year old)

Crown Prince Olav and Crown Princess Martha of Norway came to the United States on a ten-week good will tour that included a visit to the World's Fair, and spending time with Franklin and Eleanor Roosevelt at the beginning as well as the end of the tour.

The stop at the end of their tour took place at Leif Erickson

Park in Brooklyn on July 6, when the Norwegian Royals came to tour several Norwegian institutions in Brooklyn, including the dedication of the monument to Leif Erickson, in recognition of his coming to America in the year 1,000. Nearly 5,000 Norwegian-Americans, primarily from the colony where I lived, were present for the dedication, including my family. I was with them, in a baby carriage, though I only learned about these details when I was several years older. It's incredible to realize I was actually there for that event!

April 9, 1940 (when I was 2 years old)

The Germans invaded Norway in a campaign that lasted two months. They immediately took the capital of Oslo, as the royal family went into hiding. Initially, King Haakon and Crown Prince Olav tried to maintain the Norwegian government. Crown Princess Martha and her three children escaped to Sweden, and then to the United States, where they were guests of President Roosevelt—even residing at the White House until they found a more permanent home near Washington, D.C.

December 1941 through 1944 (when I was 3 through 6 years old)

Japanese planes attacked the American fleet at Pearl Harbor (Hawaii), bringing the U.S. into World War II. As a result, blackouts took place in the colony on announced dates as darkness fell during the war. This meant the large radio in our apartment, with a phonograph on top, had to be covered with a blanket when it got dark so its light wasn't visible from the street below, or the sky above our second-floor apartment. Some evenings my sister and I peeked out the front window to see if we could see any activity. We were only allowed to whisper. At times we would see one or two men—civilian ARP (Air Raid Protection) wardens—watching apartments such as ours from below. It was a scary time—especially to this preschool boy.

During these years, the rationing of certain foods took place. For a time, the commodity was sugar. Not only was the amount restricted to two pounds, but the package was limited to one per customer. I didn't understand when my mother carried two bags, gave one to me as we approached the checkout line, and said, "Here, take this bag and give it to the checkout man with this money." I did as she asked. As the man took the sugar, and the money, he simply smiled, and said, "Thank you!"

Syttende Mai – (the Seventeenth of May)

This public holiday in Norway is celebrated as Constitution Day—sometimes called National Day—with many common activities, particularly parades that focus on children in the big cities, as well as small hamlets throughout the country. The flag of Norway is flown at individual homes and gathering places of all sorts, especially the myriad flags throughout every parade. Music, singing, and ice cream commonly accompany the flag waving.

Norwegian women wear the customary *bunad,* Norway's national dress, on May 17, as well as on other special occasions such as weddings, baptisms, and confirmations. The attire varies according to the area an individual is from. However, it usually consists of a dark woolen skirt, a white blouse with a piece of jewelry called a *sølje* pinned to it, together with an embroidered vest or shawl, and a purse. Norwegian men wear *bunads* far less frequently; however, when they do, it customarily includes knee-length pants (similar to knickers), off-white socks, black shoes, and a woolen jacket with buttons made of silver or pewter.

In Brooklyn, the parade marched along Eighth Avenue. It remained there during my boyhood years (1938-1955), but later moved to Fifth Avenue, and then Third Avenue. It featured thousands of people—families, local groups, and numerous celebrities—including politicians such as the mayor of New York City, the Brooklyn borough president, congressional representatives, Norwegian organizational leaders, and, of course, the large number of observers crowding the sidewalks. It was a really big deal!

I started out in a baby carriage, then a stroller, then walking—first with my mother, later with friends, and eventually as one of many noisy observers on the sidewalk. I walked in the parade as a boy when it was held on a Saturday or Sunday. But when the date of May 17 came on a weekday, I stayed home from school and, when I was older, went swimming with other colony friends at Coney Island. Boys would go into the cold ocean water to show their bravado, while most girls watched from shore. Teachers had a hard time understanding the reason for missing school, but accepted the note we each brought since it was written and signed by a parent.

As a child I thought the 17th of May was like the 4th of July in the U.S. But I eventually learned that is not quite a clear parallel to Norway's movement toward independence from Denmark and Sweden. On May 17, 1814, the Norwegian Constitution was signed at Eidsvoll, Norway, though still under the jurisdiction of Sweden. This is the reason that date is known as Constitution Day. Then, on May 17, 1905, Norway declared its independence from Sweden. In order to maintain royal lineage, Prince Carl of Denmark became King of Norway under the name of Haakon VII.

1939-40 World's Fair (when I was 1 to 2 years old)

During these early years in my life, another festive occasion known as the World's Fair was taking place in the Borough of Queens—a place that Crown Prince Olav and Crown Princess Martha visited before they came to Brooklyn. As a memento of that celebration, my parents—who also toured the site—gave me a white, four-inch-tall plastic replica of a Trylon (a three-sided obelisk that actually reached 700 feet above ground), next to a Perisphere (a globe that was 18 stories tall), situated on top of a red, plastic base. It was seemingly unbreakable and became one of my favorite toys.

The structures themselves were located as one of the displays on 1,216 acres in Corona Park in the Flushing Meadows section of the Borough of Queens. More than 44 million people attended, celebrating the future-oriented theme: "Dawn of a New Day," with Norway and many other countries participating.

I kept the model for many years. It broadened my horizons and became my initial understanding that I was a small part of a big world—one that included Norway and the country in which I was living. My parents told me the replica was really important and that I should take good care of it. It sat in a visible place in my room during all my days in Brooklyn!

GROWING UP: BEGINNING TO IDENTIFY MY VALUES (9)

The development of my values began soon after I was born. What I saw, heard, touched, and sensed was taking place without my being consciously aware of what was happening. All sorts of feelings were emerging within me—physically and emotionally—at the same time. In addition, others were responding to me—nurses, doctors, parents, and caregivers—and they were also impacting me.

Of course, I didn't realize what was happening. But, as I was growing up, I came to understand that what started at my birth, continued throughout my life—internal experiences, and external influences. In some ways the development of my values emerged in a similar manner.

As I have already indicated, the influence of my mother was very significant in my preschool years. I experienced an attachment to her that was so strong that I behaved in ways that would please her. In other words, her values initially became mine, though I wasn't aware this was occurring. However, at the same time, I developed some of my own. For example, I valued my sense of freedom when I played outside our apartment without her watching me. She may not have intentionally thought about my developing this deep and enjoyable sense of freedom, but it continued to expand in later years as I rode my bicycle, or took the subway—always with at least one friend—all over NYC, while still in grade school. I understand this as an external influence that led to an internal experience.

Even though I had the freedom to play outside our apartment without direct supervision when I was only three years old, it was premised on our agreement: my mother setting boundaries and my agreeing to stay within them. The values inherent in this understanding were those boundaries, and the freedom that came with my playing within them.

However, how I behaved in them was not explicitly discussed. Comments like "be good" or "be kind" were made, or understood from other situations, but were general statements without any specificity. Therefore, the day I stood on my tricycle seat and tried to pull down the fire alarm handle, I didn't think of it being wrong until a stranger spoke to me—in no uncertain terms—and told me it was. I stopped, either because I had learned to respect authority, or, more likely, that I couldn't reach the handle without some help. I didn't tell my mother about it, probably because I would have been embarrassed about it. After all, she kept calling me *mama's lille engelen* (mother's little angel).

I learned many other values, particularly in my preschool years, and integrated them into my life. As far as I can remember, most of them were without negative, explosive experiences. However, I can still vividly remember one incident. It took place in our cabin in Connecticut when I was 4 or 5 years old. I can't quite recall the details that caused my father to get so distraught with me—a disposition that I don't remember seeing again—but I do recall the firm conversation on that Friday evening, after my mother told him about something I had said that wasn't true. I must have lied to my mother in response to what she asked me.

Nevertheless, after supper, my father told me I was going to get a spanking. First, we went outside to find what he called a *switch*—a slender, flexible shoot from a small tree. I didn't know what he meant, but when I saw what he picked from the tree, I got the message—loud and clear! I was really scared when we went back into the cabin. He told me to drop my pants and underpants, turn around, hold on to the chair, bend over, and not move. I was already sobbing; so was my mother. And then I felt it. Oh, how it hurt! And then again, and again. At that point, my mother told him that was enough. My father simply said, "One more time." And as he struck me again, he said, "Don't ever do that again!" I was too upset to respond. However, years later, as I reflected on this event, and the out-of-character way in which he had treated me, I wondered if my spanking might have been related to an experience he had as a boy.

I started to pull up my pants as my mother came to me, and hugged me. I was so sore. I remember getting ready for bed soon after, with all sorts of feelings—pain from the spanking, guilt for what I had done, and anger toward my father for my punishment. With my mother hugging and helping me, I slowly got into bed—crying the entire time. Finally, after I got in a somewhat comfortable position on my side, my mother gave me another tissue so I could blow my nose.

"You know you did something wrong," she said. "Are you sorry for what you did?"

"Yes," I mumbled, nodding my head.

"Do you promise not to do that again?"

Once again, I nodded, "Yes, I promise."

"Then, I forgive you. I'll tell Papa what you told me . . . and he'll forgive you too." She kissed me on the forehead, moved away from my bed, and left the room. The next morning, when I saw my father, he didn't say anything; he just took a couple of steps toward me, picked me up, and gave me a big hug.

I learned an important lesson that night to always tell the truth! In addition, the spanking—the only one I ever received—stayed with me, not only for a few weeks or months, but for the rest of my life. As a result, I've always been diligent to tell the truth, though I learned later in life that didn't mean I had to tell all the truth I knew.

I also learned two important values: consequences when I do something wrong; and, in my family, forgiveness for the wrong, when I agree to do my best not to repeat it.

Many other values also developed during these preschool years such as honesty, kindness, caring for others, sharing, helping others, and, perhaps the most important value—TRUST!

EVOLVING TRUST IN MY PARENTS (AND THEIR TRUST IN ME) (10)

From the moment I was born, I began to evolve trust in my parents. Since my mother was my primary caregiver, at home all day, she was the one to whom I initially became attached. My father was employed on weekdays, caring for the financial needs of the family, and was only at home in evenings and on some Saturdays and/or Sundays. In addition, my mother was an extrovert with a personality that was outgoing, gracious, and energized by others she encountered; while my father was an introvert, reserved, thoughtful, and sapped of energy when he had too many interactions with others.

However, both of my parents were very trustworthy! It took time, of course, to realize this, and even longer to understand it. I could depend on them to be constant in several ways. They always loved me—without exception. I never questioned that, even when I received a spanking, because there had been five years of expressing that love before I was spanked.

My parents always told me the truth. I never even thought they might not. I accepted whatever was said. As I grew in my understanding, I found myself asking questions, not to see if they were telling the truth, but to get a clearer and fuller understanding of what they were saying.

My parents were also very dependable. They lived by what they had told me, when it was what I really liked, or something I really wanted. But they also remained firm when they had given their final word on a matter I didn't want or like. As I grew older—mostly beyond my preschool years—there were opportunities for negotiating, though I learned that was supposed to take place before a decision was finalized.

These were two of the primary considerations for trust to develop in my experience, but there was also an underlying basis, namely, the secure relationship I had with my mother and father.

Security is an inborn need. Whether it begins with a primary caregiver in infancy, or is postponed until a secure attachment is formed, it is essential to experience at least a reasonable degree of security in order to become an emotionally healthy individual. Those who experience such an attachment without having to work through an anxious or avoidant attachment are very fortunate, though they don't deserve much, if any, credit for it. It is the caregiver—or caregivers—who set the tone emotionally, and provide the care to enable security to take place. In personal terms, I did not make such an attachment happen; my mother and others close to me, particularly my father who participated in my mother's actions as much as he could, deserve the credit for the wholesome attachment that emerged. I am deeply appreciative for their love, and the wise actions they expressed toward me and with me.

Individuals who do not experience a secure attachment with their initial or early caregivers, can and often do find it through one or more other persons with whom they connect. Sometimes this is another family member or friend. At other times, it emerges through a trust relationship with a therapist. In whatever circumstance this takes place, it is often an expression of what Erik Erickson, a developmental psychologist and psychoanalyst, calls *basic trust.*

The relationship I experienced with my parents from the time I was born was remarkable, particularly since they never went past sixth grade in public school, had limited resources to which they could turn for assistance, and carried out their wise care of me largely on their own. Of course, there were many friends in the church in which they were active, and the colony of which they were a part, but their parents and most of their siblings were not in this country.

One dimension was a crucial part of their daily lives: they

prayed regularly, earnestly, and fervently for my sister and me, as well as others. And in that process, they each expressed a profound trust in each other, and in God—their ultimate source of security!

This trust in God and each other permeated all activities taking place in our home. This does not mean we were an ideal home, perfect in everything we did. No, far from it! We were fully human and flawed. But the trust my parents had in God and each other never disappeared, even when it might be less evident in some situations than others. And it continued throughout the seventeen years I lived at home, as well as the years after I left, though I only experienced it from a distance, often hundreds of miles away.

This initial experience of trust in my parents led to their trust in me. When I was crawling among the branches of the fallen trees in Connecticut, they didn't watch me moment by moment; they only called out to me when they weren't sure where I was, or when they couldn't hear me humming.

In a similar manner, when I was playing on the sidewalk between our apartment and Eighth Avenue in Brooklyn, my mother glanced once in a while from the upstairs porch railing to see if she could locate me in that area. If she saw me, and noticed I was okay, she went back into the apartment, trusting me to stay within the boundaries she had set, and I had agreed to follow. I trusted her to keep her word and let me play without her direct supervision. And she trusted me to keep my word to remain in the boundary area.

I didn't think of what I was doing in those intellectual categories. No, I simply lived out my trust in her without even thinking about the subject of trust. I didn't consciously realize trust was taking place; I just experienced it.

Yes, during these preschool years, I developed trust in my mother and father, and they developed trust in me!

CHAPTER 2

GRADE SCHOOL YEARS

(1944-50)

EXPERIENCING MULTIPLE COLONIES (1)

On a Sunday afternoon in late spring of 1944, my mother and father asked my sister and me to come into the living room—an unusual request. We had never been asked to have such a meeting, and we wondered why we had been given such a formal invitation.

"I have something I need to tell you," my father began. Without sharing any background information, he simply said, "We have to move to a different apartment." My sister, 9 years old at the time, began asking questions while expressing frustration and anger. I just listened; I was only 6. And then we learned we had been asked to move. No, that wasn't quite accurate. We had been told by the man who owned the building that we had to move.

Mr. Moretti, an Italian man, lived with his wife on the first floor. He was an unusually friendly and gracious man, with black hair and pearly white teeth. He always greeted me and others in my family with a great big smile! Why would he tell us we needed to move? All I understood at the time was that members of his family were coming from Italy at the end of the summer, and he wanted them to live in the second-floor apartment. Only years later did I learn the City Council had passed a law that gave owners the right to evict renters if owners had family members coming to America who needed a place to live. That was never explained to me, in a way that I understood. I accepted the fact that we had to move.

After many unsuccessful attempts with our neighbors and other contacts within the colony, my father found us an apartment. It was located at 859 44th Street, which was 12 blocks from my first home, at the edge of the colony. It was a totally new neighborhood with only a limited number of Norwegian residents. On our street, there were almost no Norwegians at all. The people living there—I learned eventually—were mostly Italian Catholics and Eastern European Jews. Overall, they were fine people, with far more similarities to us than differences. That was a major learning for me!

Our apartment was one of 4 in the building, 2 downstairs (1 of which was ours), and 2 upstairs. It had 2 windows in the back facing a small open yard; 1 from my parents' bedroom, and the other from the living room. Two windows on the side faced a very narrow alley, 1 from the kitchen, and the other from a second bedroom. It was a very difficult place for a family of 4 to live, especially when it came time to use the small bathroom. My sister and I, who previously had separate bedrooms, struggled in that 1 bedroom since the space for 2 beds, 2 dressers, and 2 chairs left little room for anything else. The small corner closet had to contain clothes for both of us, when there was hardly enough space for one. Yet we ended up living there for 6 years.

To complicate things for my sister, she had to start fifth grade in a new school with all new friends. And now she had a brother starting first grade at the same school. I was not aware of what my sister was experiencing. I was preoccupied with my eagerness to start school.

My family and I noticed a 3 x ½ inch metal holder, tilted

vertically on the molding at the right side of the doorways into the living room and each bedroom. We weren't sure what they were, but thought they had been placed there by those who had rented the apartment before us. My father indicated he would remove them when we painted the apartment—a responsibility given to the renter. When he took them off, I was intrigued by the small letters written on the paper that was rolled up inside.

When we went in and out of the building, we noticed the molding next to the door to our apartment, to the door to our neighbor's apartment, and to the exterior door of the building itself, all had the same type of holders. My father thought they were important to the owner of the building, and that we should leave them as they were. He said he would ask the owner, who lived next door to us, what they were. He did, and we learned they were really important to Jewish people.

Some years later I learned the holders are called by a Hebrew word—*mezuzah*—a piece of parchment inscribed with the Jewish prayer *Shema Yisrael,* beginning with the words "Hear, O Israel, the LORD (is) our God, the LORD is one." The passage is from Deuteronomy 6:4-9 and 11:13-21, and contains the commandment: "Write the words of God on the gates and doorposts of your house."

Many Jewish families lived in our new neighborhood, particularly on the block where we lived. But they were not the only group. There were also many Italian families, in addition to smaller groups of Finnish, Swedish, and Irish residents in the surrounding neighborhood. This diversity was new to me, having connected primarily with people who were a part of the Norwegian colony. It became a relatively new part of my experience, particularly when I went outside to play, and even more so when I went to school and saw classmates from other nationalities, cultures, and religious traditions. It was a bit frightening at first, but soon came to be a very interesting and exciting part of my life!

In the 6 years we lived in this apartment, Elsie was 9 to 15 years old, and I was 6 to 12 years old. This age difference, coupled with ongoing struggles of growing up in the same bedroom, led to a frustrating relationship between us, though these years were more difficult for my sister. Having our own bedrooms at our cabin in Connecticut—though only 8 x 8 feet—made living there more reasonable for both of us.

BROADENING MY FAMILY (2)

Even though I had three grandparents, several aunts and uncles, and numerous cousins living in Norway, I was related to only two biological families in the U.S. One had *Aus* as their last name. Members included my mother's younger sister, *Tante Dagny*; her husband, *Oncle Olaf*; and their daughter, Martha, named after my mother. We visited with them often, especially on holidays, even though they lived north of the city in Westchester County. I called them by those names my entire life, even after I became an adult.

The other family had Hansen as their last name. They included my father's older brother, *Oncle Harold*, his wife, *Tante Clara*, and their four sons—my cousins, Arthur, Clifford, Rolf, and Roy. We visited them rarely for reasons I did not understand.

On one occasion in 1947, *Oncle Olaf* was remarkably excited to tell me about the Norwegian explorer, Thor Heyerdahl, who, on April 28, 1947, had just completed his voyage from Peru (in South America) to Polynesia aboard a raft named *Kon Tiki.* He demonstrated that the ancestral roots of Polynesians were not based solely in Southeast Asia, but also in South America.

Oncle Olaf was a well-read man. He cited news releases, and later gave me a copy of the book named after the raft—a story so exciting that it even became a movie that circulated theaters world-wide. He also told me about other Norwegians who were early adventuresome explorers. The one I remember most was Roald Amundsen, who not only navigated through the Northwest Passage, but also was first to reach the South Pole on December 14, 1911.

We celebrated holidays, especially Christmas, with *Tante Dagny, Oncle Olaf,* and Martha—often at our apartment. My mother loved to decorate, with the tree as the focal point. It was always an inexpensive one, purchased close to December 24 to get a lower price, sometimes needing a branch—even two—where there was a bare section. She placed strips of cotton to the branches to resemble snow, and dangled tinsel all over the tree. Norwegian ornaments hung on the tree in many locations, often with a *julenisse* (Christmas elf) included in one or more places, and a layer of cotton as the skirt for the tree that included a mirror to resemble ice, with miniature colorful skaters on it. When we visited several other homes during the season, no Christmas tree was as attractive as our tree—which was not only my sentiment, but that of most others who came to visit us.

We would often hear Christmas and other seasonal music in our home, from the radio and 78 rpm records, or from members of our extended family and friends. At other times we listened to a musical instrument such as a violin, guitar, or harmonica. Similar sounds echoed at homes we visited in the colony. At Bethelship Church, we often walked around the Christmas tree and sang carols in Norwegian as well as English—sometimes in double lines going in opposite directions to accommodate as many people as possible. Norwegian seamen from ships in the harbor would sometimes be picked up by church members and brought to our Christmas festivals, providing a place for them to celebrate with others from their home country.

Foods were also important at Christmas. In addition to a special plate in our homes that included nuts with a fancy nut-cracker, figs, and dates among fresh fruit, there was a variety of homemade baked goods, served in our church as well as our homes: *Julekake* (Christmas bread), *smultringer* (donuts), *sandkaker* (sand cakes), *krumkaker* (thin, flaky cakes), *peppakakor* (pepper flavored gingerbread cookies), and marzipan figures. Most important was *riskrem* (cold rice pudding mixed with whipped cream), served with a sweet red sauce.

Sometimes my mother would secretly place a shelled almond nut in the *riskrem*, with the individual who ended up with it getting a prize. Then, one year at our home, after my mother served that dessert, and we all had finished eating, no one announced that they had gotten the almond. I grabbed the big serving spoon, ran it through the remaining dessert, to no avail. It simply wasn't there. I quizzed my mother to make sure it had been put in the pudding. She verified she had included it. I believed her, but wondered—out loud—what had happened to it. We looked at each other's plate, and couldn't find the nut. After sharing all sorts of ideas regarding what might have happened, *Oncle Olaf*—almost unnoticeably—put his hand to his mouth and out came the almond. With a wry smile he asked, "Is this what you're looking for?"

Christmas Eve, rather than Christmas Day, was the primary time to celebrate. Families gathered for a festive meal and the exchange of gifts, mostly for the children, after dinner. It was common in our home for my mother and father not to receive gifts except for small personal items my sister and I bought for them, as well as for *Tante Dagny*, *Oncle Olaf*, and Martha. These might include a comb, handkerchief, pad of writing paper, or special bar of soap.

One year my sister and I asked my father why he hadn't bought a nice gift for my mother. He responded by saying gifts were for children. In order that we wouldn't ask the same question the following year, we found a gift under the tree with my mother's name on it. We were momentarily pleased until she opened it and we learned that it was only two pairs of hosiery. What was even more bothersome was that she had gone out and purchased them, wrapped them, and put her name on the tag. She didn't feel it was right to spend money on herself when we didn't have much money.

I sometimes wondered if we would run out of money since our only source was my father's job. And then, one day, as I was thinking about money, I wandered into my parents' bedroom to ask my father a question, I found him looking through the top center drawer of his dresser. It was not simply open, but had been taken out of the dresser and placed on the bed. I stood there, puzzled, and momentarily forgot why I had come into the room.

"Are you wondering what I am doing?"

I responded, "Yes."

"I thought you would eventually find out. I just didn't know when."

He went on to show me a small horizontal drawer that went in first, before the larger drawer went in. No one who would look for money in the drawer would ever find it. My father kept some of his cash there. It was also where my mother could go if she needed cash to go to the store, or whatever. Yes, it was an ingenious and secure location for a limited amount of money, especially since he didn't have a checking account, and credit cards were not yet available. His mantra was: "If you don't have the money, don't buy it!"

While talking about money, my father told me about Bay Ridge Savings Bank, on Fifth Avenue and 54th Street, where a person could safely keep money, and even have the bank pay interest on it. Soon thereafter, he took me to the bank, gave me two dollars, and had me open a savings account, in order to learn that my money could increase if I would leave it there for the bank to use. I was glad to learn that I could eventually take it all out. As a result, I began to learn the importance of saving money and earning interest on it!

During these grade school years I also learned to use certain expressions in Norwegian:

God dag.	"Good day."
Takk for sist.	"Nice to see you again." (literally, "Thank you for the last time.")
Hvordan står det til?	"How are you?"
Jo takk, bare bra.	"Very well, thank you."
Uff da.	"I am sorry to hear that."
Er du gal?	"Are you nuts?"
Ja.	"Yes."
Nei.	"No."
Hallo.	"Hello."
Adjø.	"Good-bye."
Har det godt.	"Best of luck." (literally, "Have it good.")
På gjensyn.	"See you again." (like *Au revoir* in French)
God natt.	"Good night."

FINDING ADDITIONAL FRIENDS (3)

Moving to the edge of the colony meant fewer Norwegian families lived in our neighborhood. Almost everyone I met had a last name that sounded Italian, Jewish, or some unrecognizable ethnicity. Days, even weeks went by, before I heard the name Jacobsen—likely a Norwegian or Danish name, since it ended in *sen,* while *son* would probably be a Swedish name. And the way I found out was through my conversation with Clifford, a friend from Bethelship Church. He had heard I had moved, and that I lived closer to where he lived—on 43rd Street, between Seventh and Eighth Avenue. We became close friends, but we were in different first-grade sections at school.

Those who were in my class had no Norwegian last names—a totally different group of children my age. It took a while to get to know them, but I soon learned those who were Italian (most of the class), or Jewish, or some other nationality, were not very different from me. We learned and had good times together during school hours, but we had most of our fun in the games we played in the neighborhood, especially when we were a little older, and could go outside, or to each other's apartments.

One student in my fourth-grade class whom I liked a lot was Mary. She was really smart, got high grades on almost everything. She also had an engaging smile—especially when our eyes connected with each other—and a laughter that was genuine and contagious.

I was invited to her birthday party in the spring of that year. I accepted her invitation, and when the day came—on a Saturday—I walked up the street to her apartment with a box of candy in hand, rang the bell, and went into the living room that already had several boys and girls from our class. I knew everyone who was there, or who would soon arrive—all

Italians except me. Mary's mother and another woman were also there, and were incredibly gracious to us. Before long, we sat down at two long tables, ate some small sandwiches, and drank some root beer soda. Then Mary's mother brought in a cake with nine pink candles brightly burning, as we enthusiastically sang "Happy Birthday, dear Mary!"

After eating, we played some quiz games while the mothers cleared the tables. Then Mary's mother got our attention and said, "Have fun. My friend and I will be upstairs if you need us." We thanked them for the food as they left, and sat around the living room, talking and joking with each other. A few of us went into the den. After several minutes went by, we suddenly heard Mary, in a very loud voice, say, "Where's Adolf? I want him in here!" I was stunned as I got up and walked toward Mary who was smiling with bright red, thick lipstick covering her lips. She smiled and said, "Come here, next to me. I'm going to give you a kiss you will never forget." Everyone cheered, even shrieked, with laughter. And then it happened. She just said, "Turn your cheek to me." I did, and her lips started on my cheek, slid down over my jaw, and down my neck to my collar. My classmates cheered and applauded. Mary took a step back, smiled, and laughed more joyfully than I had ever heard her.

After kissing a couple of other boys sitting near her, she turned to one of her girlfriends and asked if she wanted to put on some of her mother's lipstick. Without any coaxing, she smeared on some lipstick, and kissed a boy. Mary, however, was quick to get the lipstick back, and commented, "I don't want my mother to be upset that I used too much of her lipstick."

I went searching for a mirror to see what I looked like, and then some tissues to wipe it off. Mary said, "Come into the bathroom and I'll help you get it off." We walked down the hall, as did a couple of other boys, and we wiped and wiped. I wanted to get it all off before I went home. I kept wondering what my mother would say if she found out.

After a lot of struggling, Mary called her mother, explained what she had done, and asked for her help. Her mother didn't seem pleased with Mary, but saw the predicament I and two other boys were in, and came to the rescue with cold cream—or whatever else she used. Finally, she said, "I think I got it all. I don't think your mother will even know about it, unless you tell her." I told her it actually was a lot of fun. She smiled in return. So did Mary, who was standing next to her.

After the party was over, I went home and told my mother it was such a fun party, though I didn't tell my mother that I—the only Norwegian at the party—had become a star! However, later in the evening, when I took off my polo shirt, I noticed the lipstick mark on the edge of my collar. I didn't know how to get it off, so I simply showed my mother, and let her know Mary was playing a game and got some lipstick on my neck. I didn't tell my mother she was kissing me. My mother didn't ask any further questions. I was so relieved. She just said, "I think I can get it out."

I also continued finding additional friends at church in Sunday School, in Cub Scout and Boy Scout troops of which I was an active member, and in a Weekday Religious Education Program for boys and girls in fourth, fifth, and sixth grade. It met at Trinity Lutheran Church on Fourth Avenue and 46th Street, the last hour of the school day, every Wednesday afternoon.

I was developing a sense of community, both within and beyond the Norwegian colony!

BEGINNING MY SPIRITUAL JOURNEY (4)

The sanctuary in Bethelship Methodist Church in Brooklyn was filled with children and youth, as well as parents and other adults. It had been a festive atmosphere for children during the entire Sunday afternoon. As a closing event, we sang songs, heard a Bible story, and listened to Mrs. Davidson, a very gracious woman, telling us that Jesus wanted to come into our lives. She led us in singing the song: *Into my heart, into my heart, come into my heart, Lord Jesus. Come in today. Come in to stay. Come into my heart, Lord Jesus.* Then she invited those of us who wanted to invite Jesus into our hearts to come forward and stand in front of the circular altar rail, as we sang the song one more time.

I understood enough of what she was saying—even though I was only 6 years old—and I responded, as did a number of other children. Those of us who had come forward were led—line by line—in a brief, unison prayer, before we returned to our seats. It was not a highly emotional experience. It was, however, my opportunity to invite Jesus into my life.

A couple of years later I received my own Bible and, at the encouragement of my mother who was thrilled by my decision, I printed these words on the opening page: *When i was 6 YEARS old i GAVE MY HEART To JESUS* (written here exactly as I recorded it). I was just learning to write in school—using upper and lower cases was still not clear to me, having had limited instruction at school, and no such instruction at home. I followed up on this decision by taking a keen interest in learning about Jesus at home and at church.

In May 2018, when I traveled to Brooklyn from Indianapolis to visit locations from my childhood and to interview friends with whom I had grown up, I had dinner with three couples in one of their homes. I asked them for their recollections, and shared some of mine. When I talked about this event at church, Ellie shared with us, "I was also at that service in 1944 and went forward as you did." I was stunned!

Before I could respond, Ruthie added, "I was there too,

and also went forward." I could hardly believe it. Three of us—74 years later—recalling that event, and sharing its significance throughout our lives as disciples of Jesus Christ. Wow! What a joyful surprise!

That decision at 6 years of age stayed with me in the years that followed, since I saw those words—over and over again—every time I opened my Bible to the first page. As a result, I continued to reflect on this experience, wondering if *inviting Jesus into my heart,* and *giving my heart to Jesus,* were different experiences; or, simply different ways of describing the same experience. One was an act of receiving; the other an act of giving. I concluded, thanks to several discussions with my Sunday School teacher, that the experience was the same, but its meaning was worth further reflection.

I was reminded of these questions when I attended junior high school. I thought of my experience as a six-year-old when I began learning about the human heart in biology class. With an inward smile, I asked myself, *Did I invite Jesus into my right auricle? Or my left ventricle?* Of course I never told anyone about these thoughts, but I did wonder. Was my experience just a childish understanding that took these words literally—an event I should now relinquish? Or, was it something more? I wasn't sure. I thought I would just set it aside for the time being and not spend any more time thinking about it.

Having looked at the image of Jesus painted on the front wall of the chancel area in the sanctuary every Sunday, and the portrait of Jesus that my parents had in a frame in our living room, I often wondered what he might have looked like. My mother thought the image we had at home was a wonderful representation. She didn't use big words like that; she simply referred to the image as *Jesus.* When I would ask if we really knew what Jesus looked like, she would admit that we really didn't know, but that image was Jesus for her. She loved it! And because of her strong emotional connection, I identified with it too! At that time in my life, I hadn't seen any other representation.

Years later, a friend was visiting us in our apartment, and noticed the image of Jesus on the wall, and asked me a question: "Do you like the picture of the Norwegian Jesus?"

Having never thought about that connection, I didn't say anything. He added, "That picture is very popular with Norwegian people." I don't remember what I said, if anything at all. But it certainly made me think!

Several years thereafter, I visited Pilgrim Pines, a resort owned by the Evangelical Covenant Church (formerly the Swedish Evangelical Mission Covenant Church of America), and viewed a collection of original paintings by the Swedish artist, Warner Sallman—all representations he had named *Jesus, Head of Christ.* I more clearly understood why my mother and father and many of their relatives and friends loved his most popular image of Jesus, with its long brown, wavy hair, and elongated Nordic forehead. It is an image that has been used in numerous Sunday School publications throughout a large number of Protestant denominations.

I continued my spiritual journey by going to Sunday School, and attending worship services with my parents and my sister. At home I learned to pray extemporaneously at bedtime, usually kneeling at my bedside. And I gave thanks to God at every meal time—though my sister and I joked about whether we had to pray or not, when we only had a snack. We also had family devotions (reading from the Bible, briefly discussing what we read, and praying) on some Saturdays when our family was together. I still remember my father repeating the same phrase almost every time he prayed: "We thank you, God, that we have everything that we need."

PLAYING OUTDOORS IN AND BEYOND THE COLONY (5)

The neighborhood where I grew up during my grade school years was composed of apartment buildings, mostly two stories in height. Some were attached row houses; others were individualized townhouses; still others were structures of limited heights such as the four-story structure next door to the two-story dwelling in which I lived. Wrought iron fire escapes were visible all over the front of the building. However, on some of the avenues connecting the streets, there were stores—lots of them! Eighth Avenue was a prime example.

A candy store filled with comic books, newspapers, magazines, Spauldeens, and a phone booth, as well as candy, peanuts, bubble gum with baseball cards, ice cream, glass bottles of soda, and a soda fountain, was often located on one of the four corners of an intersection, like the one at Eighth Avenue and 44th Street. Also common on an avenue was a number of grocery stores, as well as meat or fish markets, drug stores, restaurants, taverns, clothing stores, and ethnic shops with collections of sweaters, cookware, and curios of all sorts.

There were also many other establishments (as identified in the third Appendix). Older children and youth played in the side streets where traffic was light and moved in one direction. The use of chalk was ubiquitous! A large piece of white chalk—1 inch in diameter, and 6 inches long—was the favorite because it showed up well on the black top covering most streets. Lines marked the bases in stick ball, goal boxes in hockey, and boundaries in a variety of other games. Scrawled messages rarely contained nasty words. Drawings were frequent, some being outstanding artistic renditions, particularly faces of people!

The most common sight on the streets was a group of boys

playing a game with a Spauldeen, manufactured by the Spalding Company. When it produced tennis balls, some didn't have enough of the fuzzy stuff for the outside of the balls, so the company shipped them to New York City and sold the bright pink, unused rubber cores as the *Spalding High-Bounce Ball,* all over the city. The kids who got their brand-new, pink Spauldeen for 25¢ loved the aroma—the smell of Bazooka bubble gum. It was a marketing stroke of genius!

We didn't have baseball fields or any other kinds of fields. We had smooth, blacktop streets, where legendary games that often included a Spauldeen took place. You could whack it and send it for what seemed like a mile, but it almost never broke anything. In addition, we had a limited number of so-called playgrounds: slabs of concrete surrounded by cyclone fences.

During these grade school years I played on such a fenced-in concrete slab at my school, PS 169, more often than in the street where I lived. If someone had a stick, we'd play stickball. The stick might be a handle from a mop, a carpet sweeper, an old broom handle, or a dowel stick from the coat closet. Sometimes we would draw a box on the wall and fill it in, so we would be able to tell if it was a ball or a strike—no chalk was a ball, and chalk on the ball was a strike. If the batter hit the pitch, he ran the bases. If he hit the ball over the fence, it was a homer.

Occasionally we would go to a friend's house and play stoopball with the Spauldeen. One of us—usually a boy—would firmly throw the ball at the peak of one of the steps in front of the house, and as the ball came back, those in the field would try to catch it on a fly for an out. If it bounced once, it was a single, twice a double, and so on. At still other times, we tried to play stick ball in the street, though I, and most others in grade school, weren't very good at it. But did that ever change when we went to junior high school. It became a passion for most boys!

When it came to inventing games with a Spauldeen, the only limit was our imagination. Sometimes we played a variety of handball games against a concrete wall. At other times, we placed a coin on the thin crack between two slabs of concrete in the sidewalk. Then, if two were playing, each of us stood back at an equal distance from the coin, and bounced the ball in an attempt to move it toward the opposite side.

Games at this age also included striking, and then keeping, marbles of competitors in the street next to the curb or in a dirt lot. We also pitched pennies (at times higher value coins) against a building wall. The one who came closest was the winner of all coins thrown. We roller skated in the street, and sometimes held onto a milk wagon led by a horse pulling it. We played *tag-you're-it,* either while running, or roller skating, or by spitting hard peas through a large plastic straw.

In cold weather there were indoor games, parties, and a variety of other activities. But in the winter of 1947, when I was 9 years old, action took place outdoors when snow started falling on the afternoon of December 26. It snowed and snowed all afternoon, throughout the night, and continued the next morning. When it stopped, 26.4 inches had fallen (as recorded at Central Park in Manhattan). The entire city was completely paralyzed, stranding buses and cars, even shutting down the subway system. What a great time we had during the seven weeks that the snow lasted!

Bicycle riding became one of my favorite outdoor activities in the warmer seasons. I started riding a two-wheeler early—at age 6 or 7—because a bicycle shop was located only a block away. The first time I went with Clifford, one of only a few Norwegian friends in that part of the colony. His apartment was a couple of buildings from the shop. He knew the person who worked there—a very kind man who had visitors sitting on a bike in two minutes.

After a few explanatory comments, particularly how to stop, by pushing the pedal backward, the man said, "You can take it outside for a few minutes and try it on the sidewalk in front of this building. I'll be out there too, if you need me." I could hardly believe it. I don't remember saying anything. I just got on, struggled to balance it at first, and actually let it roll on a slight incline, and even applied the brakes. It was such a thrill! I was so proud!

Clifford, who was also starting first grade in a few weeks, called out to me, "See, I told you it wasn't hard to ride a bike!"

I agreed and asked the man how I could rent a bike. He answered my questions, and added, "As you can see, I have many different sizes in bikes. You can move up to bigger ones whenever you're ready." I couldn't wait to get home and tell my mother, and especially my sister, that I had learned to ride a two-wheeler, and was now ready to rent a bike. I also wanted my father to know when he got home from work, so I could lay the groundwork for getting a bicycle of my own.

He was pleased that his boy was growing up, but said to me: "Son, we can only afford one bike, so you'll have to wait till you can ride a big one." What a motivator to learn how to ride a 26-inch two-wheeler. (By the way, no one ever wore a helmet.)

So many things happened in my neighborhood during my grade school years. One event turned into a very formative experience. It began one morning when I was walking toward Eighth Avenue. One the guys living on my block called out to me as he headed across the street. Holding up some round pieces of metal, he exclaimed:

"Look, Adolf, I found these at the construction site down the street. They look like nickels, don't they?" He handed me one.

"What are they?" I asked.

"I think they must have been knocked out of those boxes electricians use. They were laying on the ground in a trash heap—lots of them! Let's see if they'll work in the peanut and gumball machines." We walked to the corner where the machines were located. "Let's try one," he said, inserting a slug. Out came a handful of peanuts. "What a neat discovery!"

After eating a few peanuts, and then a few more, I replied, "I have to go." I knew this wasn't right. I walked home very slowly, thinking about what I had done, and wondering if I should tell my mother.

"You don't look well," my mother said as I came in the door. "Are you alright?" I started to cry. "What happened?" I told her the whole story, my words punctuated with sobs. She listened quietly. "You understand that you did something wrong?"

I nodded, "I'm sorry."

"I forgive you because you said you were sorry." We hugged, then she added, "Now, go into your room and ask God to forgive you."

Oh no! I don't want to tell God what I did, I thought. *God already knows what I did.* I knelt down at the edge of the bed and asked God to forgive me. When I went back to the kitchen, my mother greeted me with open arms.

"I forgave you; God has forgiven you; now take this nickel and go to the candy store, tell the man what you did; tell him you're sorry, and give him the nickel."

"But, Mom, I said I was sorry, and you forgave me. I told God I was sorry, and God forgave me. Isn't that enough?"

"No, you have to give the man the money for the peanuts."

I took the nickel she gave me, and headed out the door. What should have taken me a couple of minutes took me a lot longer. I thought about all sorts of ways not to tell the man what I had done. However, several minutes later, I went to the store, saw the door was open, waited to make sure no one else was in there, and entered. In a matter of seconds, I blurted out that I had put a slug in the peanut machine, had gotten a handful of peanuts, was sorry, and was giving him a nickel for what I had taken without paying for it. I spoke so rapidly, I don't know if he fully grasped what I tried to say, but he got the point. I simply laid the nickel down on the counter. He was stunned, and told me I could keep the nickel for being so honest. However, I left it on the counter. It was his, not mine!

I left so quickly I don't remember anything about my walk home. I felt so relieved! Seeing my mother with a smile on her face when I returned, led me to smile as well. In the days that followed, I thought about what I had done, how my mother had responded, and the way I had carried out a path to forgiveness and restitution. I had learned some important lessons!

DEEPENING RELATIONSHIPS IN THE SECOND COLONY (6)

I cherished my time outdoors in Brooklyn, though many of my best times outdoors were in Connecticut. Both of these settings were connected to *friluftsliv* (literally: *fri* or free, *lufts* or air, *liv or* life)—not simply as a word, but a lifestyle, grounded in a cultural heritage! It encompasses the significance, not only of the outdoors, but of bonding with nature. And the summers in New Fairfield, Connecticut, made this possible to a much greater extent than the neighborhoods in Brooklyn. I didn't know the word *friluftsliv* when I grew up—my parents never used it, and may not have known it—but I knew the experience. I lived it, especially in the summer, as well as on those many weekend trips!

The concept of *friluftsliv* first appeared in Norwegian literature through the writings of Henrik Ibsen. One was in a poem, *On the Heights* (1859); the other was in a play, *Love's Comedy*

(1862). In both of them, Ibsen deals with the experience of a free life in communication with nature and its impact on the development of one's physical and spiritual well-being. It's the key to living a happy life in Norway, and consequently, in the U.S.

An additional part of this lifestyle for me was the freedom that went along with the interaction with nature. My parents did set a boundary for my exploration in the environment surrounding not only our home, but the entire area as far as the eye could see—up the hills behind the house, and through the vast woods beyond the stone wall at the edge of our property. And the boundary my parents set was this: *You are free to go anywhere, as long as you can still see the house.* Did I feel a sense of freedom? Wow, did I ever! I not only loved it, but I also tested it to see how far I could go—by myself as well as with someone else. It was a long distance!

The properties in Connecticut were surrounded by heavily wooded lots, with a brook running through them, and a huge number of blueberry bushes scattered throughout the hillsides. On the way to the lake—a body of water, 11 miles in length, and 2 miles at is widest point—there was a constantly running spring of clear, cool, drinkable spring water. A variety of wildlife such as deer and foxes, and numerous birds of all sizes, shapes, and colors, permeated the entire area.

Many in this second Norwegian colony were like one big family. The adults—called aunt (*tante*) and uncle (*oncle)*—and their children, called by their first names, were my functional family. They included Elsie (my sister), Ruthie (who lived next door), and Arthur (her brother). Farther down the road were Karen, Eleanor, Marilyn, Judy, Johnny, and Skippy.

Activities that were most common included visiting each other's homes, hiking in the woods (with and without paths), climbing trees, building huts in the wooded areas of our property, and sloshing around the brook. Others were playing games of all sorts, eating meals with other families, gathering around campfires, and, of course, swimming in Candlewood Lake—often without lifeguards or adult supervision.

When I was in grade school, our cabin, named *Cozy Nest* by my mother, had no electricity, no running water, no bathroom (only an outhouse), no heat (only a fireplace), no electric iron (only a ceramic/metal-faced iron heated on a stove). We did have an ice box large enough for two huge, rectangular pieces of ice purchased at the ice house. We kept them in a large wooden, homemade ice box that we opened rarely and closed quickly. Outside we had two 55-gallon drums, connected together to catch rain water for all uses except for drinking.

Our outhouse was our only toilet, and we used it each day regardless of the weather. Only during nighttime hours did we use a pot under each bed. It was convenient, but we had to empty it every morning. When I had to go to the bathroom during evening hours, and it was already dark outside, I would sometimes let my mother know I was going to use the *tissepotten* (pee pot) under my bed, even though it wasn't night time yet. Rather than tell her, I would sing the beginning of a ditty she taught me:

Me: *Mama, jeg skal tisse.* (Mother, I have to pee.)

Mother: *Skal du det min ven?* (You have to do that, my friend?)

Så gå hen til sengen, og ta tissepootten frem. (So go to your bed and take the peepot out.)

The text continues with another verse and a chorus, but this sample illustrates one of the many amusing conversations I had with my mother.

Occasionally we saw vehicles on the gravel road that led to our driveway. Sometimes a relative or friend stopped by for a visit. When they did, they usually parked on the road and walked up our steep driveway. On one occasion, a young man in a bright yellow convertible, with his date cuddled close to him, tried to step on the gas and drive up, thinking it was a continuation of the road. He got stuck in the gravel, spun his wheels several times, and eventually had to back all the way down to the road. At other times trucks came, usually to deliver building materials, though sometimes to sell milk, ice cream, and other dairy products, or to hawk fresh vegetables from the farm.

With limited cultivation of gardens in these early years, other children and I often meandered through all sorts of wild shrubbery and greenery on the hillsides surrounding our homes. Sometimes undesirable results took place. One such recurring event was the poison ivy we inadvertently touched. Without knowledge about a treatment that would heal the effects of it on the skin, or stop the spread of it, my mother told my sister and me that she had a way to successfully deal with it, but that it would hurt, and maybe hurt a lot; but the itching would stop, and the pimples would dry up in a day or two, with only one application.

"What do you have to do to make it go away?" we asked.

"I have to rub it with Clorox on a piece of cotton," she replied.

"Clorox?"

"Yes, and it will hurt; but only for a short time." After some agonizing conversation, we agreed. Mother did what she needed to do. We screamed and cried as the undiluted bleach broke through the skin; but in a short time, the pain stopped. By that evening, and the next day, it was gone. I decided I would try not to get poison ivy again. I really tried, but I somehow got it again. Did I get the Clorox treatment again? Yes, I did. Even a few more times. But I survived!

However, that was not the only difficult experience I had. On another day, while several of us were playing in some tall weeds not far from Ruthie and Arthur's house, one friend let out a blood-curdling scream, followed by others yelling at the top of their lungs! I don't remember the sequence, but I do remember the anguish! Three others and I had inadvertently stepped on a hornet's nest on the ground. We didn't know this until we felt the intense pain in our arms, legs, and thighs. Two of us who were wearing long pants tore them off, since the hornets had crawled up our legs. Both of our mothers came running, knowing something terrible had happened. In a matter of seconds they were getting dark dirt from the ground, mixing it with their saliva, and putting the paste on our bites. And, while doing that, they were telling us to do the same. Our crying subsided, but the pain lingered for some time, especially for those of us who had multiple stings.

Other remedies for bruises and scrapes often came from a drugstore. We regularly used mercurochrome—a general antiseptic that I, and most of my friends, wore all over our bodies in the summer—and, when necessary, iodine. Also, those of us in Brooklyn purchased from a Norwegian druggist named Halvorsen, two types of salve he made: one for healing the skin, and another for drawing out whatever was problematic under the skin.

We also had lots of fun! One activity was going deep into the woods to pick blueberries, and sometimes digging up, and bringing back, a small hemlock, or mountain laurel bush, along the way. This was an activity *Tante Dagny* loved more than anyone else in the colony. We sometimes waited until she was coming to stay with us for a few days before a group of families would go in late morning with our picnic lunches, lots of water, and a container in each of our hands—a coffee can for each child, and a bucket for each adult. When adults weren't watching, the children ate more blueberries than they put in their cans.

As we returned to our cabin, some of us put our berries in *Tante Dagny's* bucket until it was nearly full. Why? Because she would swing the bucket in front of her, and then behind her, over and over again, a little higher each time. We watched and waited, and then—suddenly—she would swing the bucket up in circular fashion, over her head, and down to complete the circle. Thanks to centrifugal force, she never lost a blueberry. When those of us who were children wanted to try, she said, "Ok, but you'll have to try it with water." She showed us first, and then several of us children tried. It was hilarious! Most children got wet; some were drenched! But a few of us finally learned, after a few tries.

Another venture we included almost every time we went swimming, was a stop at Green Light, a restaurant with ice cream specialties of all sorts. An ice cream cone was not fully satisfying unless it was at least a double-decker. But that was not all. For some of us, the height of satisfaction was playing a game of pinball while trying to keep the ice cream from dripping on the floor, and winning one or more free games!

An additional fun-filled experience was our visits to an old abandoned house that a group of us discovered—without adults present—on one of our exploration walks in a wooded area off the main road, in the opposite direction from the lake. It started out as an intriguing path into a wooded area since it appeared that a dirt road might have been there decades earlier. Without trees laying across the path, we walked until we could no longer see the road behind us. Suddenly, coming out of nowhere, we saw a house that might have been inhabited many years earlier. We were startled and frightened! We stopped, became silent, and just looked—all around us. Slowly, we began to walk toward this dilapidated structure, our hearts beating faster and faster! As some of us peered through windows, we saw some old furniture, but mostly dirt, dust, and lots of cobwebs. As all sorts of scary thoughts raced through our heads, we heard a bloodcurdling scream. Not being sure whose voice that was, we started to emit shrill, piercing sounds as we ran through the path we had just sauntered along a short time before.

We regrouped when we arrived back on the main road, imagining all sorts of wild possibilities. Did we want to explore that house further? Perhaps, but not on that day. We were too scared. We talked, laughed, and made up all kinds of stories on our way back home. By the time we arrived, we had tentatively decided that we did want to go back someday. In the meantime, we decided to call it *The Spooky House.* (And, yes, we did go back that summer and others—over and over again—especially when we had friends from Brooklyn visit. And did we ever scare them! It was so much fun!)

LEARNING IN GRADE SCHOOL – PUBLIC SCHOOL 169 (7)

Since kindergarten was not available, at least not in the area of Brooklyn where our family was living at the time, I had to wait until I was 6 to enroll in first grade. My mother, sister, and I walked from our apartment—only a block and a half away—to the main entrance of a huge, five-story building, covering all of 43rd to 44th Street on Seventh Avenue. I was filled with excitement; my sister seemed somewhat subdued, which surprised me because she loved school. What I didn't realize was that she was enrolling at a school where she didn't know anyone, having completed the first four years at P.S. 105 in the neighborhood where we used to live—in the center of the Norwegian colony.

I enjoyed school from the beginning. My teacher, Mrs. Nelson, was so gracious. She created an atmosphere in which I, and others in the class, felt remarkably comfortable—even on the first day. None of my classmates were Norwegian, but that didn't concern me. They were all so friendly. Each of them smiled when they looked at me and the other students; I did the same. We learned as a group from the start. This was new for me, since my sister and I were far enough apart in age that our learning was not with each other. Furthermore, my mother and father could only speak English in minimal ways, and often turned to Norwegian when they spoke to each other. I thoroughly enjoyed learning with, and from, others in the class.

Although I did unusually well in spelling at school—regularly becoming the winner of the class spelling bee—I struggled with reading comprehension. It took me years to recognize this limitation, and relate it to the fact that my mother, who couldn't read English, was unable to read stories to me as a child. Consequently, I had almost no books at home. At the same time, I learned penmanship as well as anyone in my class, using the Palmer Method that was illustrated in both upper and lower letters across the top on the blackboard at the front of the room—a style of writing that I can still use, but hardly ever do.

Through grade school I also performed well in many subjects, especially math, though I also excelled in social studies, music, drawing, and citizenship. By the time I was in sixth grade I had academically excelled to the point where I, and some others in my class, took a set of exams to verify accomplished learning as well as potential for the future. Although it took me a while to grasp the implications of what teachers were explaining to those of us who had achieved high scores on those tests, I eventually understood that I was being offered the opportunity to complete 3 years of junior high in 2 years.

My parents received a letter announcing this program and were excited by the offer. I wasn't as excited at first, because I thought it meant school would get a lot more difficult—completing 1 ½ years of work in 1 year, and then repeating the academic load for a second year. But with a more comprehensive understanding, I came to appreciate the honor of being invited into such a program. Of course, my parents assumed that we would accept this opportunity. We eventually did, and overall, it turned out to be a great experience!

I was not entirely surprised I was invited, once I learned of this program, since I had earlier received unusually positive comments from some of my teachers. One such example comes from 2 letters my fourth-grade teacher sent to me at our summer cabin in Connecticut (letters I still have because my mother saved them).

The first one, dated June 30, 1948, began with this sentence: "Congratulations on having the best report card in the class." My mother read it to me more than once the day I received it. She was pleased and surprised, not being aware that I had excelled to that extent in my class. But I was surprised too, because I didn't realize I was at the top of the class in this manner. There were more than 20 students in the class, and I thought one among several others would have the best report card, but not me. I had learned to listen carefully, and work diligently in class, knowing that if I did, I would have less homework. However, when necessary, I also studied at home.

Many other experiences permeated my life in grade school. One was the frightening exercise we had to go through several times in first grade. Since WW II was taking place primarily in Europe during 1944-45, the teacher and other individuals from the government trained us to take cover in case of an air invasion. They gave us directions on ways to protect ourselves if any threatening situation would take place. It included getting down on the floor next to our desks, and then moving under them in a kneeling position, with our heads held down, and covered by our hands. What was scary was the awareness that it might really happen, though Mrs. Nelson assured us that it was unlikely, and told us not to worry about it—an instruction easier to understand than to follow.

A second experience was the enjoyment I found from playing the violin, beginning at age 7 with a three-quarter size instrument my parents bought for me. This was my father's desire, that I would learn to play as early in life as I could. Lessons began with the most basic instructions (how to hold the violin, move the bow, place the fingers on the strings, and so forth). The resulting sounds, though tolerable to me, were horrible to my sister, and wonderful to my parents—especially for my father, who had always wanted to play the violin himself, but that aspiration never came to fruition. I graduated to a full-size instrument after a couple of years, and continued to take lessons throughout grade school, and into junior high school. I did well enough to join the school orchestra, and to play solos at church, particularly during the annual Christmas programs. By the time I entered high school, the violin had found its resting place in the hall closet.

Numerous other activities took place across the street from the school in Sunset Park—25 acres of recreational buildings nestled among cultivated grasses, shrubs, and trees nestled between Fifth and Seventh Avenues, and 41st and 44th Streets. Retaining walls surrounded the edge of the park since most of the park was higher than the streets. In addition, a substantial section of the park sat on top of a 164-foot hill that is part of a moraine (a ridge made up by an irregular mass of boulders, gravel, sand, and clay left by a glacial drift). Such an elevated location, one of the highest in Brooklyn, provided views of the New York Harbor, the Statue of Liberty, and Manhattan, as well as the shoreline of Staten Island and New Jersey.

In my grade school years I sometimes played in the center that dominated the eastern side of the park, the area closest to

P.S. 169. It included sporting fields, a magnificent bathhouse, a large rectangular pool (265 by 165 feet) with a depth of 3.5 feet, and two semi-circular 165-foot pools at either end. One had a depth of 12 feet for diving, with boards at two heights: 1 meter (3.25 feet), and 5 meters (16.4 feet). I jumped off the lower board frequently, even dove off it. But I only had the courage to jump off the highest one a few times. Jumping off the high board was considered a coming-of-age event, particularly for the boys. A limited number of girls also jumped.

I had a lot of fun playing on a snow-covered walkway in the winter, the one that became quite steep from Sixth to Fifth Avenue. It was known as "Dead Man's Hill." Stories told every year indicated what had happened in a prior year to a guy racing down that hill on a sled, splitting his head open when he hit the chain link fence at the bottom of a long set of stairs, at the point where the stairs made a 90-degree turn to the left. Everyone swore that it really did happen! I wasn't sure it occurred the way it was told, but each time I made that sharp turn—without a helmet—I was scared my head might hit that same fence. Nevertheless, it was so much fun! Scary too. As if that wasn't enough, it was even better when a coating of ice had fallen. The ride was faster still!

An event in the park that turned out to be frightening took place one evening as it was getting dark. I was walking on a roadway in the park, approaching the corner of 44th Street and Seventh Avenue, when a group of high school guys called me over to where they were standing. I didn't know any of them, but thought I'd better respond since there were five of them and only one of me. They seemed friendly and asked me to do a favor.

"What do you want me to do?" I asked.

"See that girl and those three guys over there?"

"Yeah."

"They're friends of ours, and we want to have some fun. Go and ask the girl this question: 'Can I park my car in your garage?' And then come back here."

I didn't understand the question, but I went thinking this was going to be something for fun. I came up to the group, looked at the girl, and said, "Can I park my car in your garage?" All of a sudden, the guy next to her yelled and lunged at me, as I turned toward the guys I had been with, and ran as fast as I could. Glancing over my shoulder, I saw the guy chasing me with a shiny switchblade in his hand, poised to stab me with it. At that moment, two of the guys I was with grabbed him and, after an intense struggle, stopped him, saying, "Don't hurt this guy; we set him up to do this. We thought it would be funny."

Then the guy still holding the knife in his hand asked me, "Do you understand what you were saying?"

"No, I just said what they told me," I responded. I don't recall what else was said, but the guy yelled at me as he returned to the girl he was with. The guy who sent me over indicated he was sorry for what happened. I took off as quickly as I could, looking over my shoulder a few times on my way home. I didn't tell my mother or anyone else what had happened. I also didn't understand the sexual implications of what I had said until several months later.

ENGAGING IN ACTIVITIES BEYOND SCHOOL (8)

Throughout the fall, winter, and spring, I spent most of my after-school hours outdoors, either playing in the street or in the school yard. During the summer months from Memorial Day through Labor Day, I lived in Connecticut, where the woods and the lake were my outdoor playgrounds.

Other important locations were the parks in Brooklyn. In

addition to Leif Erickson Park and Sunset Park, Prospect Park was the location of choice. It was far enough away that riding a bicycle was the only practical way to get there. This was not a problem, since my parents had given me a full-size 26" bike for my tenth birthday—a promise they made to me on the day I first rode a small two-wheeler.

That gift had a dramatic impact on my life. It provided a way for me to go anywhere I wanted to go—or so I felt—even though deep down, I knew that was a feeling, not a reality. However, it was a very important sentiment, because it gave me a sense of incredible freedom that I had never before experienced. It went beyond setting boundaries (what I had been taught in my earlier years), since my mother was unsure about what boundaries to set. I didn't consciously realize it at the time. I don't think my mother did either. But that former framework was no longer practical, not even possible!

She changed her approach, and asked more questions: "Where are you going?" she would ask. And," When will you be back?" And, "Who are you going with?"

At first, I tried to answer these questions, but I soon realized I couldn't easily answer the first two. I would say, "I'm not sure exactly where we're going, but I'll be back . . . ," and then gave her an approximate time indication like "in time for supper." And then I always let her know with whom I was going. That became our pattern, though it often turned into letting her know I was not going by myself. I liked what I regarded as our agreement since I also didn't want to venture into many areas of Brooklyn by myself.

My first lengthy bike ride was a trip to Coney Island when I was 10 years old. I went with Clifford, who was helpful in figuring a way to get there, and home again. I remember feeling thrilled, yet somewhat overwhelmed with all the sights. The boardwalk—on which we could ride our bikes—was 80 feet wide and stretched for nearly 3 miles. We rode and looked, and looked some more, vowing to come back!

My favorite bike rides were to Prospect Park: 586 acres, filled with not only the most beautiful landscaping I had ever seen, but also a sculptured bust of the Norwegian composer, Edvard Grieg. In addition, the park had a marvelous zoo that included elephants, rhinos, seals, sea lions, bears, monkeys, lions, and wolves. There were also numerous restaurants, pools for swimming, lakes for boating and fishing, and fields for sports of all types—plus horseback riding in the warmer weather, and ice skating in the winter. Together with one or more friends, I visited the park frequently since it was only a short bike ride away.

One evening during these grade school years I went to Ebbetts Field for the first time with a friend of my father, who understood baseball unusually well. It was the home field for the Brooklyn Dodgers. Our seats that night were along the third base line. It was incredibly impressive: the size of the stadium; the cheering crowd when the Dodgers got a hit, and even louder when they scored a run. The expressions of exuberance and joy (by most, though not all, of the fans), when Jackie Robinson came onto the field was most exciting, particularly since he had broken the color barrier on April 15, 1947—only a few weeks before this game with the St. Louis Cardinals. I fell in love that evening—with baseball, with the Dodgers, and with Jackie Robinson, whose photo hung on my bedroom wall until I graduated from high school and went away to college.

My parents also did special things in the city with my sister and me, though it was uncommon, since my father went almost every weekend to Connecticut. However, on one occasion I clearly remember, my mother and father took Elsie and me—by car on the way to visit relatives—to see Macy's

Thanksgiving Parade. It was a total surprise, one that we didn't know a thing about until we parked the car on a side street in midtown Manhattan, and started walking toward a crowd of people along the sidewalks. It was a delightful experience I will never forget!

The most significant events of this time in my life took place in 1945 at the end of World War II—when I was 7 years old. The war had started on September 1, 1939, the day Hitler invaded Poland. It had developed further when Germany occupied Norway on August 9, 1940; and still further when Americans entered the war on December 7, 1941, after the Japanese bombed the American fleet in Pearl Harbor (Hawaii). And it concluded in phases, the first one on May 8, 1945.

This day in May, called V-E Day (Victory in Europe Day), was the day the German Nazis surrendered unconditionally in defeat, the day the Nazi occupation in Norway ended. As a seven-year-old, I didn't understand what actually happened. But when my parents heard about it in Connecticut—at a picnic gathering of our family, the Bensens, and other Norwegian friends, they were overwhelmed with joyous excitement. All I remember was Arthur, a three-year-old who lived next door, climbing on top of the large, wooden table, with some remains of our meal still there, and jumping off. No one hollered at him, so I climbed up too, and jumped down. We did it again since no one had stopped us the first time. But we didn't press our luck. We didn't try it a third time.

On August 14, 1945, an armistice was signed when the Japanese accepted the terms of the Potsdam Declaration. This day became known as V-J Day—Victory over Japan Day.

On September 2, 1945, Japan formally surrendered, officially ending the war in Asia—a war that continued for 6 years and 1 day.

On October 27, 1945 (Saturday), the American World War II ships came into the harbor in midtown Manhattan.

On October 28,1945 (Sunday), my father, together with my mother, my sister, and me went to the location of those ships and climbed on board two of them: first the "USS Missouri," and then the "USS Enterprise." Little did I know this day would become one of the most important days of my grade school years!

The "Missouri," also known as "Mighty Mo," was an enormous battleship. It was 887 feet in length (almost as long as three football fields), with a beam of 108 feet, a height from keel to mast at 209 feet, a weight of 58,000 pounds (at full load), and a speed in excess of 30 knots. Americans admired it greatly because it was on the deck of this ship that the Japanese signed the Formal Instrument of Surrender. My father told me we were going to visit that ship and make an attempt to see that brass plate. I didn't really understand what he was telling me, and I couldn't even begin to comprehend the significance of what he was saying. But I could tell it was really a big deal for him. He spoke to me with such deep feeling. I knew he thought it would be very special!

We got up early on that Sunday, and left by subway to get to Manhattan. Eventually, working our way through the throngs of people, we saw the ship tied up to the pier. I was excited beyond description. We stood in line for a very long time. Finally, we got to the front of the line. I was nervous, wondering if the officer on duty would let us board the ship. He had turned away so many people ahead of us. But I remembered my father telling me that he thought they would let us get on board. I had believed him when he told me, because he always told the truth.

Then the officer looked over the special paper my father had given him, looked directly into my father's eyes, and simply said: "Welcome aboard, Mr. Hansen!" And then the officer turned to my mother, my sister, and me and said, "And welcome to the members of your family!"

I asked my father how he knew who we were, and how the paper got us approved. He showed me the paper, and the place at the top where the word *PASS* was printed. He then explained that the battleship was built in the Brooklyn Navy Yard (aka New York Navy Yard) where he had worked during the war as a cabinet maker in the officers' quarters. I was so proud of my father for having been chosen to do this special work!

I learned that the ship was launched on January 29, 1944, and commissioned on June 11 of the same year. It had arrived in the Hudson River on October 27, 1945, 8 weeks after the Japanese had surrendered aboard the ship, and I was now looking at it—yes, only 8 weeks after that surrender. Wow!

After we got on board, and slowly worked our way to the actual location of the big brass plate, I found it difficult to realize where I was standing, and even more difficult to understand that the words I was looking at was the actual text of the agreement. Then an officer called all the people who could hear his voice, and asked everyone to be quiet as he read the inscription: "Over this spot / On 2 September 1945 / The Instrument / Of Formal Surrender / Of Japan To The Allied Powers / Was Signed / Thus Bringing To A Close / The Second World War / The Ship At That Time / Was At Anchor /In Tokyo Bay"

Everyone applauded and cheered when he finished.

It was soon time to leave and move on to another ship—an aircraft carrier—called the "USS Enterprise." After we followed a similar process for boarding, we headed up to the main deck. When we got there, I stared at the far end of the deck. It went on and on—as far as I could see. It seemed like the end was a mile away. After looking around in every direction, my father and I walked, hand in hand, the full length of the ship. There was so much to see as we walked and looked—walked and looked. *Wow* was all I could say to myself. It was so massive. Planes were incredible; cannons were gigantic; masts pointed so high into the sky. I felt so small, but strong enough to keep going as I felt the big hand of my father holding on to me tightly, or at times, my hand holding tightly on to his. This 20,000-ton carrier had an incredible history, which I learned some years later. It had chased the war for more than 275,000 miles. Its planes and guns had shot down 911 Japanese planes, sunk 71 ships, and damaged, or possibly sunk, another 192.

To a seven-year-old, it was an overwhelming day. My father was more emotional than I had ever seen him. My mother also—often had tears in her eyes. These ships represented the entire six-year war, including the landing of American and other Allied troops on Norwegian soil a few months earlier to defeat the German Nazis!

Our family was so deeply engaged in what we experienced—the sights we saw, the sounds we heard, the things we touched, the odors we smelled, the excitement we felt, and the myriad thoughts that kept racing through our minds—all in the midst of a crowd much bigger than I had ever been a part of. There was so much I couldn't grasp, so much I couldn't understand, so much I couldn't even put into words as to what was going on. The enormity of it all was so powerful. Yet I still remember so much of what took place that day—October 28, 1945. I will never forget it!

GROWING UP: DEVELOPING MY VALUES (9)

In my preschool years, my parents set boundaries to limit my freedom. In Brooklyn, it was "stay on the sidewalk, and keep between our apartment (on 56th Street), and the corner (Eighth Avenue)." In Connecticut, it was "go anywhere, as long as you can see our cabin." At first my mother monitored them, but when she saw that I was playing within them, she trusted me to continue, and stopped watching me. She may have kept an eye on me, but that seemed to lessen over time. As I've already indicated, I felt a great sense of freedom.

However, when the option of boundaries was difficult—sometimes impossible—both my mother and my father resorted to other means of helping me deal with my freedom in responsible ways. Without their articulating what they were doing—perhaps because they were not cognizant of it, or couldn't express it in English—they began increasingly to turn to values rather than rules. Looking back at their actions and their comments from my current perspective leads me to a deep appreciation for the ways they helped me mature.

I didn't understand the distinction between values and rules, not even the meaning of these words. But I did grasp that their effect worked for me as well as them. For example, rather than set bedtime hours when I was in grade school, my mother would simply say, "I think it's time to go to bed soon." And she would say it in a tone of voice that made it sound like she was asking if I agreed. Or, that's how I took it. I would sometimes respond, "Ok;" and at other times we would briefly talk about why I thought it was not yet time. She would often conclude with these words: "You need your sleep." That was the value.

This pattern continued until I left home and went to college. I understood the value, and was never given a bedtime. I tried to work it out so I would get the sleep I needed—sometimes, however, less than what my mother thought. After my grade school years, I was never given a time to be home in the evening. I was simply told, "Don't stay out too late!" I think I probably followed that guideline closely enough that I don't recall ever hearing: "You stayed out too late last night." They might have asked other questions—either when I arrived home, or the next morning—but they were not about the time I came home. In other words, I generally didn't live by rules at home. I lived by values. However, had I not stayed within overall boundaries that both my parents and I thought were reasonable, they might not have given me the freedom to decide when to come home.

In my preschool and grade school years, boundaries functioned like guardrails on a road. They kept me from going off the edges while, at the same time, giving me freedom to make choices. Sometimes—perhaps most times—I enjoyed the freedoms without consciously thinking, or even realizing, the presence of boundaries. When I went bike riding within and beyond the colony, my mother would assume I would be going with at least one friend because that was the agreement we had. She didn't have to say, "Go with someone," because she knew I would. She might say, "Don't go too far," or, "We're planning to have dinner at 6," or, "Be careful," or some word of encouragement like "Have a good time." But there were no rules to repeat.

Looking back over these early years, my perception is that the values I inculcated into my life were what I *caught* from my parents and other members of the Norwegian colony, not what I was *taught*. I resonated with the way of life I was experiencing to such an extent that I could continue to take responsibility for my life—commensurate with my age—and find fulfillment and enjoyment in whatever I did. Did problems arise? Certainly, but there were also solutions that could be worked out. Overall, I really enjoyed my grade school years!

DEVELOPING TRUST IN OTHERS (AND THEIR TRUST IN ME) (10)

I learned the meaning of trust in my relationships with my mother and father. I trusted them, and they trusted me. I wasn't able to articulate what I was experiencing, but I understood what it meant in life situations.

During my grade school years I developed meaningful trust relationships with others in the colony, both in Brooklyn throughout the academic year, and Connecticut in summers. One of the most significant relationships was with my immediate family living in the United States. This included *Tante Dagny*, my mother's younger sister, with whom my mother had been close her entire life; *Oncle Olaf*, her husband; and Martha, their daughter who was 10 years older than me. Even though they lived in Rye, New York—about 50 miles north of our home—we were together for all the major holidays, as well as other family celebrations.

In addition, I had scores of functional aunts, uncles, and cousins in the colony. I can't think of any of them that I didn't trust during those years. And that wasn't unique to my personal experience. It was the common sentiment among almost everyone I knew, especially those with whom my parents also connected. Many of these relationships were fostered by our mutual participation in the life of Bethelship Norwegian Methodist Church.

One way to describe this quality is in the words "social trust"—a central quality of the entire Norwegian colony in Brooklyn. However, I never heard these two words used together until my adult years, when I became aware of this quality of life in Norway. I learned that social trust was replete throughout that country—particularly in those parts where the people were still largely homogeneous. In addition, I also ascertained that this type of trust was prominent not only in Brooklyn, but in the lives of Norwegians living in colonies all over the world.

During my grade school years, my experience of trust extended to children and adults who were not Norwegian. As

I became acquainted with them, I transferred the qualities of trust that I had been developing. This became an enriching part of my life as it broadened my relationships. My peer relationships in school and on the streets, supplemented those from church, my former neighborhood, and those with individuals in Connecticut.

The counterpart to my trust in others was their trust in me. I not only enjoyed this part of my experience, but found it to be encouraging and strengthening. I learned I could depend on others, as they depended on me. And this applied to adults as well as children. As I trusted parents of my friends, they trusted me. Likewise with my teachers at school—and at Sunday School, both in Brooklyn and Connecticut—and other adults with whom I connected. I couldn't articulate that this was taking place, but I did sense a closeness that I not only liked, but anticipated in ways that enabled me to grow in my maturation.

Learning to trust others also led me to navigate the world successfully. I grew in self confidence in a number of areas in my life as I trusted others. At the same time, I also lost some of my immaturity, naivete, and credulity. I was learning how to question, to avoid trusting too readily, especially without adequate evidence. But that was a slow, ongoing process that needed assistance from more experienced friends. I listened to those I felt I could trust. Sometimes that worked well; sometimes it didn't. At times it even became a stumbling block. However, as I look back, I was in the process of developing street smarts—a process that still continues today, as I find myself in new places and circumstances!

CHAPTER 3

JUNIOR HIGH YEARS

(1950-52)

CONNECTING WITH A PEER COLONY (1)

In the late spring of 1950, my parents were overjoyed that an apartment had become available in the center of the Norwegian colony at 932 56th Street, just one block from our first apartment in Brooklyn. My sister and I were pleased we could move back to our former neighborhood. The landlord was a Norwegian family named Larsen.

We spent our time that summer in divided locations. We made a number of trips to Connecticut, sometimes for a week or two, other times for a weekend. The schedule was confusing and frustrating, but when we were approaching Labor Day, the anticipation of my starting a new school, and my sister living closer to her school, created a sense of excitement! I would be attending Pershing Junior High School; my sister would be returning for her sophomore year at Bay Ridge High School.

When I walked to the corner of 56th Street and Ninth Avenue on that first Monday morning of school, I saw a group—all girls except for one boy—gathered next to the black, wrought-iron fence surrounding a two-story house. I didn't recognize any of them, but they looked like they might be Norwegian—light-skinned, blond hair, with one of the girls wearing a *lusekofte* (Norwegian sweater). I crossed the street and, as I took a few steps toward them, one of the girls said "Hi." I don't remember what we said after that, but I do recall their smiles and friendliness.

This was the first time I was with a group of friends from my immediate neighborhood. It felt good, even comfortable, though I didn't know any of them. They seemed well acquainted with each other. At the time, I didn't realize that they had probably all attended the same grade school—P.S. 105—located nearby. I learned later this was not the only reason they already knew each other. Most of them attended the same church—59th Street Norwegian Evangelical Lutheran Free Church—and had spent years attending Sunday School, summer camps, and other activities throughout the school year.

That morning marked the beginning of my peer group—a type of relationship I had not yet experienced. Not only would I connect with those with whom I walked to school, but with many others I met once I arrived at school. What became particularly interesting, and subsequently deeply meaningful to me was my becoming part of a Norwegian peer group. At the same time, being part of a school that was not predominantly Norwegian; for my homeroom class had relatively few Norwegians in it.

Almost all of my closest friends at this time in my life were approximately the same age, had Norwegian parents with a similar cultural heritage, lived by the same basic values, and demonstrated a deep sense of trust toward one another. Up to that point in my young life, I had never been part of such a cohesive group. It was new, exciting, and fulfilling. I was more content than I had ever been with any other relationships I had developed. Part of that experience was my age, and the social needs I had at the time. Little did I, or my parents, realize how critically important this was to my maturation, and how difficult junior high years must have been for my sister.

Most of the peer group lived on 56th, 57th, and 58th Streets, between Eighth Avenue and Fort Hamilton Parkway (another name for Tenth Avenue in this section of Brooklyn). This meant we often saw each other outside of school, particularly on Saturdays, Sundays, and holidays. Their surnames were sometimes *patronymic* (inclusive of the first name of father or mother)—Hansen (son of Hans), or Hansdatter (daughter of Hans); or *toponymic* (inclusive of a location—land, berg, or dahl). Common were names such as Buckstad, Egeberg, Gundersen, Haanes, Hansen, Heie, Helgesen, Holmgren, Holvik, Jacobsen, Knudsen, Larsen, Mathisen, Morch, Nilsen, Olsen, Osthus, Pedersen, Ringdahl, Samsen, Samuelsen, Sollie, Svendsen, and Tjornholm.

First names—also called "given names"—of friends in the neighborhood included some common American names, and others that were typically Norwegian. Boys' names were Birger, Borge, Einar, Ivar, Kaare, Kjell, Leif, Odd, Rolf, Sven, Thor, and Victor. Girls' names were Astrid, Bjorg, Clara, Hardis, Ingeborg, Ingrid, Kirsten, Lillian, Lita, Mabel, Ragna, Solveig, Swanhild, Thelma, and Turid. My name, Adolf, was not in sync with other Norwegian names. Friends would often ask about the origin of my first name, and when they understood my father's name was Adolf, they didn't ask for a further explanation. However, one of my friends gave me the nickname, *Adee* (with a long *A*), though we would spell it with two numbers: *80*. Later in life, I sometimes wrote my name as *A. D. Hansen,* since I didn't have a middle name.

We had many commonalities. For example, the favorite drink of my peer group—particularly the boys—was a chocolate egg cream. It had neither eggs, nor cream. It was made with milk, seltzer water, and chocolate-flavored syrup (Fox's U-bet—considered the most authentic syrup). I loved it! A common recipe was as follows: Pour the syrup into a tall chilled glass; carefully add 1.5 to 2 inches of milk; put a long-handled spoon in the glass; tilt the glass; add the seltzer, carefully cushioning its flow with the spoon to create the foam; then stir vigorously. Or, add the seltzer before the syrup to make the foam white (the more common way in many places in Brooklyn).

Other popular drinks included sarsaparilla soda, birch beer soda, and root beer soda (flavor supposedly coming from a root). They were somewhat similar in taste. Mallomars (chocolate covered graham cracker base, with a creamy marshmallow type of filling) often accompanied the drinks.

FINDING AN EXTENDED FAMILY (2)

Tante Dagny, Oncle Olaf, and Martha made up the inner circle of my extended family. They comprised the biological family that my parents connected with, not only in the United States, but also in Norway, particularly in Arendal, where *Tante Dagny* and my mother grew up. It also was an important family for me, particularly for the delightful times I had with my cousin, Martha. She was 10 years older than me, and often did fun things with me, as if I was her younger brother.

One experience I vividly remember was when I was 13 years old, spending the weekend with Martha and her family. Her father, *Oncle Olaf* to me, had just purchased a new 1951 Kaiser with a stick shift. She took me downstairs to see their new sleek-looking, shiny gray car, parked on the private road that led to the coach house on the grounds of the Coveleigh Country Club in Rye, N.Y., where they lived. She opened the door to the driver's seat and said, "Jump in. I'll go to the other side." Then she said, "Here are the keys. Go ahead and start it." I did. Next, she asked: "Want to drive?" Before I could answer, she said, "Have you ever used a stick shift?" I indicated I had not.

The instructions began: "There's a clutch on the floor . . ." and continued for several minutes, when she said, "Well, it's time to try it." I followed what she told me as best I could, but kept racing the motor, lurching forward, stalling, and starting over and over again, eventually doing better, but not very smoothly.

And then, unexpectedly, the loud voice of *Oncle Olaf* thundered as he walked toward us, "Martha, what are you doing? That's a brand-new car!" I don't remember what anyone said next. All I remember was Martha turning off the motor and getting out of the car. I also got out and walked away as quickly as I could. Later, when I saw Martha, all she said was, "We had fun, didn't we?" She smiled. So did I.

My parents really enjoyed being with our biological family. They trusted them as well as many individuals in the Norwegian colony, particularly the parents of the peer group of which I was a part. This led not only to a depth of relationship among group members, but also a mode of interaction that included individual and group visits to one another's homes. It would not be unusual for me to go to a friend's home unannounced—boy or girl—to ask if he or she was home; or, to have a friend come to my home. We did this frequently, any day of the week throughout the year. It felt like I was going to a second home!

The parents of these close friends were functional aunts (*tantes*) and uncles (*oncles*) to me. I never considered that I didn't have the right to go for a visit; I assumed that was an unwritten understanding. If my friend was eating lunch, I sometimes would be asked if I had already eaten; if not, I would be offered a place at the table. Comments by a mother busy with other activities would often be: "If you want some more lemonade, Thelma will get it for you;" or, "Help yourself, there's more in the fridge." Sometimes, when the friend I came to visit wasn't home, I might be invited to come in anyway. The colony at times seemed like one big family, with small subgroups connecting at deep levels of interaction.

Foods served in homes in the colony were often similar.

In addition to the baked goods that were eaten at Christmas time, there were others such as *grislebrød* (gristle bread), *bolle* (rolls), *fyrstekake* (flaky shell with almond filling), *melkekake* (milk cake), *knekkebrød* (crisp bread, sometimes called hard-tack), *flatbrød* (thin flatbread), and *kringle* (ring-twisted bread with fruit and/or raisons). Other foods included *lapskaus* (thick stew of diced or minced meat, potatoes, onions, and other vegetables), *fårikål* (lamb and cabbage stew), *kalvesus* (jellied veal), *lutefisk* (cod cured in lye), *kjøttkake* (meat balls), *fiskepudding* (fish pudding), *gjetost* (goat cheese, or brown cheese), *nøkkelost* (caraway, cumin, and clove spiced cheese), *rullepølse* (cold cuts), and several kinds of herring.

Most of the homes in the colony were blends of Norwegian and American cultures. For example, some families disciplined themselves to speak English all the time; many used a mixture of the two languages; a few spoke predominantly Norwegian. Some families dressed in clothing that gave no indication of a Norwegian heritage; many included occasional items that reflected their background; a few identified with their ancestry as much as possible. Other degrees of the blending of cultures were evident in the words they spoke, the decorative furnishings in their homes, the activities they carried out, the places they went, and so on. But evident in most families was the ongoing adaptation to an American culture.

Infused within the colony were circles of social trust, beginning with the immediate family, and continuing to broader biological connections, and then to functional ones. However, it didn't stop until it included most of the colony in Brooklyn, and eventually the remaining pockets in this country and the world, particularly in Norway and the other Scandinavian countries: Sweden, Denmark, and Finland. Numerous studies have shown that a high level of happiness has often developed when social trust has been combined with high levels of social equality and economic productivity, as evidenced in these countries.

Naomi, my wife, and I have visited these four countries, but only for a couple of days each, except for Norway where we spent two weeks in the summer of 1996—one week by car in southern Norway visiting my relatives in their homes, and one week with a Norwegian tour group in the fjord country, visiting families in the central part of the country. We also spent another two weeks of learning in the summer of 2009, traveling with our daughter, son-in-law, and two grandchildren by ship along the coast from Stavanger to Honningsvag—above the Arctic Circle—and back south to Bergen.

Prior to those visits, and subsequently since, I have studied the people of Norway to supplement the understanding that I experienced through the perspectives of my parents and others during the 17 years I lived in the Norwegian colony in Brooklyn (1938-1955). The congruence of these sources has been remarkable. They have deepened my comprehension, and enhanced my awareness and discernment in ways that have provided insightful perspectives on my personal heritage.

Yet the most impactful influence of the central meaning of the Norwegian-American family came to me from a book titled *Mama's Bank Account,* written by Kathryn Forbes. I was only five and couldn't read it when it was published in 1943, but four years later my mother purchased a copy and started to read it—a task that was difficult for her. My sister also read it, and told me about it. I decided I also needed to read it, which I did, though it was a slow process for me, having been exposed to very few books. I was so intrigued because it seemed like *Mama* in the story was just like my own mother—my own *Mama*.

The book is a fictionalized drama about second-generation Norwegian immigrants in San Francisco—also the location of the author's home in her growing-up years. The warm-hearted ambiance of the book resembled my family, and many other families in the Norwegian colony of which I was a part. The story deeply affected me when I became aware that no bank account existed after all! Wow! What a surprise! What a *Mama!*

The book was sufficiently popular on a national scale that it inspired a successful play, a television series, and a movie titled *I Remember Mama* in 1948 (when I was 10 years old).

CULTIVATING RELATIONSHIPS WITH FRIENDS (3)

Social trust among those in our peer group continued to develop during my years in junior high. This was particularly important for me since I was new to the group. I hadn't lived in the neighborhood in prior years; neither had I attended grade school with any of them. I had moved to my new apartment only a few weeks before school started. And, most distressing to me, was that almost all of those who met on the corner to walk together to school were going into eighth grade. I was entering a class called *7-8 Special 1.* How would they respond? Would they think of me as a seventh grader? Or, a potential eighth grader? That really bothered me, though I kept those thoughts and feelings to myself.

Not much time passed before they asked me a lot of questions—not judgmental ones, but inquisitive ones. When they realized I would be completing ninth grade the following year, and would graduate with them at the same time, they moved in the direction of accepting me as *one of them!* That was an incredible gift to me. They would tease me about being a special person, but quickly realized I was no different than them, though I was younger than some of them.

The peer group—loosely defined as a group because those

who came to an activity varied to some extent—consisted of both boys (often called guys) and girls (sometimes referred to as gals). Most of the times spent together were informal gatherings in one of our homes. We told a lot of stories; ate some wonderful snacks; sang a variety of songs, with or without instrumental accompaniment (some related to our churches, and others from varied sources); and played games of all types, often humorous, sometimes hilarious!

One game demonstrated an expression of *social trust* (though I didn't understand this at the time). It involved a rather innocent form of kissing. It was called *This One, That One, or The Other One.* Our group of junior high guys and gals sat in a circle on chairs, or on the floor, in a living room. One person volunteered to close the door and go into the next room. Then a volunteer stood up, and pointed to three people of the opposite sex, seated at varied places in the circle, saying to one of them, *this one;* to another, *that one;* and to a third, *the other one.* Group members often made comments—often in whispered tones—to others close by.

Then, the person leading the group opened the door and said to the person in the other room: *This one, that one, the other one.* Without knowing to whom the leader had pointed, the person in the other room called out one of these three choices. The person chosen left the room, went to the room where the person making the choice was located. They embraced and kissed, taking as little or as much time as they wanted. Comments from the group often ensued, loudly enough for others to hear them, mixed with a lot of laughter. The two in the next room returned; the one initially in the other room became the new leader, and chose a new person to go into the next room. The process continued until everyone had a chance to participate. Anyone who had not been called was given two or three of the titles so he or she would be included.

Not only did everyone take part, but the choice was unknown to the person making the decision. This meant the group was spontaneously responsible for one another's well-being. Although minor in significance, it was another expression of the social trust that existed among those in the peer group. It was also a ton of fun!

However, there were also times when it was one guy meeting one gal. For me it took place in Lillian's apartment on 57th Street, only a block from where I lived. We were both in the same general science class, and had received our unit notebooks with comments and a grade. Lillian had received a lower grade than the A that I had gotten. We shared our grades with each other, but didn't discuss them. Without being aware that Lillian had shared both of our grades with her mother, I learned from my mother that Lillian's mother wanted me to come to her apartment so that I might help Lillian raise her grade. I responded to my mother that getting together was fine with me—especially since I really liked Lillian—and she could work out a time for us to meet. We connected one afternoon the next week. I brought my notebook.

When my mother and I arrived, Lillian's mother looked over my notebook, liked what she saw, and sent us off to Lillian's room. Since there was no couch, and no comfortable chairs we could place next to each other, Lillian suggested we sit on the floor, on the far side of the bed, and lean our backs against it. We did that, and started paging through, with Lillian inquiring and I responding about the process I had developed.

The way we were seated put us close enough to look at the same pages together. As our arms touched, we looked at each other, and smiled. We talked a bit, and looked down at the pages. Then we looked up again, talked some more, smiled, looked into each other's eyes, and giggled. Without thinking about what I was about to do next, I moved closer and kissed her. After seeing her beautiful smile, I kissed her again, and again. After a few minutes of not looking at the notebook, we were startled as we heard Lillian's mother talking in a loud voice from the doorway behind us, "Lillian, I thought you were going to learn from Adolf and the way he organized his notebook."

Before Lillian could answer, I held up my open notebook over my head. "Here it is; we're studying it," I said. I don't remember what else was said, but we moved apart, put the notebook between us, and continued going through it—all the while smiling and giggling as quietly as we could. Soon thereafter, we went back to the living room, and Lillian told our mothers we had finished. My mother and I said goodbye, and left. On the way home, my mother said nothing about our kissing—I'm not even sure she knew about it. She only commented on what a nice girl Lillian was.

The next morning on the way to school, I walked with Lillian and we reminisced about the day before. When I asked if her mother said anything about our kissing, she said, "No, I don't think my mother was bothered about that. She was concerned about what I had learned that would give me a higher grade at the end of the next six weeks. She's always pushing me on my grades!" I was relieved to hear that, but I was more excited about the fun I had kissing a girl more than once—for the first time in my life!

In the weeks that followed, I often walked with Lillian to and from school. I sometimes carried one or two of her books—a visible sign that a boy liked a girl. I even wrote notes to her on the inside of the brown paper bag we used to cover our books. And then the day arrived when I secretly purchased an ID bracelet and had my first name engraved on it. Since it was customary for a guy to give a gal his bracelet as a symbol of going steady, I walked her home one evening soon thereafter. As it was getting dark, we stopped under a large tree before reaching her home. I gave her a kiss, and asked her to go steady with me. I offered her my bracelet, which she took right away, and put it on. She gave me a goodnight kiss, and headed home.

I couldn't wait for the next morning when our group would meet on the corner of Ninth Avenue and 56th Street. I hadn't told anyone about the bracelet. I wanted them to see it first on Lillian's wrist. But I was shocked when I saw Lillian walking toward me with her head down and her left hand clenched. She asked me to take a few steps away from the group, and held out her hand. "When I showed my mother the bracelet, instead of being happy, she told me I was too young to go steady, and I would have to give it back to you," she said, "I'm sorry. I really wanted to wear it." I was stunned. I don't remember what I said or did; I simply joined the group and headed to school, thinking: *I'm not too young to go steady; after all, I'm a teenager—13, almost 14!*

DEEPENING MY SPIRITUAL JOURNEY (4)

During my two years in junior high, I related to four churches in the vicinity of my neighborhood. One was Bethelship Norwegian Methodist Church (located at Fourth Avenue and 56th Street), where I was baptized as an infant, attended Sunday School in my preschool and grade school years, and was confirmed in junior high. A second one was the Norwegian Evangelical Lutheran Free Church (located on 59th Street, close to Eighth Avenue), where most of our peer group were members. A third was First Evangelical Free Church (located between 65th and 67th Street, close to Sixth Avenue), where others attended. A fourth was Second Evangelical Free Church (located at the corner of Eighth Avenue and 52nd Street), where still others affiliated. The shortened names for these churches were Bethelship, 59th Street, 66th Street, and 52nd Street.

Each of these churches were *free* churches, even the Lutheran one. What this meant was those who worshipped in these churches wanted to distinguish themselves from the Lutheran state church in Norway—a way of understanding *church* that was familiar to them when they lived in Norway. Each of these congregations had services in English and Norwegian (both Sunday morning and evening) in the 1940s and '50s. It's interesting to note that the Church of Norway became an independent legal entity on January 1, 2017, after having been the state church of Norway (i.e., the public religion of the nation) ever since the Protestant Reformation in the early sixteenth century.

I had been attending Bethelship all my life, but I became increasingly interested in attending 59th Street after my move back to 56th Street. I was planning to be confirmed at Bethelship, but was beginning to reconsider. My parents were still quite active at Bethelship and assumed I would continue to be. They were not pleased with the possibility of my leaving. We continued to discuss this matter during my initial year in junior high. We came to an agreement that if I would remain at Bethelship, attend Sunday morning worship, and go through class instruction to be confirmed in my second year in junior high, I could thereafter change my membership and join 59th Street. In addition, they were fine with my participation in the youth programs at 59th Street right away. I was confirmed on May 4, 1952, but in the months that followed, became inactive in that congregation. The following year I joined 59th Street.

The theological understanding and practical application of the Christian faith was quite similar in these two churches, as well as the other two Evangelical Free Churches. The focus was on personal salvation, a perspective that I experienced and learned to deeply appreciate. At the same time, and subsequently throughout my senior high years, I became increasingly uncomfortable with what seemed to me to be an almost exclusionary focus on individual faith. We sang numerous songs with the oft-repeated pronouns *me, my,* and *mine.* For example, *My Jesus, I love Thee, I know Thou art mine.* I was not negative toward this usage; I liked the words. I sang them with deep meaning. However, at the same time, I felt Jesus was for many people, not just me. I sometimes would think how meaningful it might be to sing, *Our Jesus, we love Thee. We know Thou art ours,* though the grammar would need to change.

I particularly thought of the use of pronouns when we would say the Lord's Prayer: *Our* Father . . . Give *us* this day *our* daily bread . . . Forgive *us our* trespasses . . . Lead *us* not into temptation . . . deliver *us* from evil. No individual pronouns! I knew Jesus was teaching a group of disciples in his ministry, but he spoke these words to large crowds of individuals that had gathered to listen to him.

I also heard so much emphasis in these churches on personal salvation that it seemed to exclude, or at least diminish, caring about the physical, emotional, social, relational, and economic needs of people. This struck me as I saw the needs of people, and related that to my study of the life of Jesus, especially in Sunday School and other youth Bible studies. I found Jesus not only concerned with leading people to love God, but to love their neighbors as they loved themselves. As a result, I talked a lot with pastors, youth leaders, the proprietor of the Christian bookstore on the corner of Eighth Avenue and 51st Street, and youth in our peer group, as well as others interested in discussing these issues.

A meeting place that brought together youth from these four churches was Dodenhoff's Ice Cream Parlor. Common times to get together included gatherings after a weekday evening youth meeting at 59th Street, anytime on Saturday, and after the noon meal on Sunday. Most of the youth who came had a strong faith and were united by a deep spiritual bond. I was often present; I could easily walk there. We had so many good times at that place, both indoors when there was room, and outdoors when it was crowded.

My spiritual journey blossomed during my junior and senior high years: 1950-55. A highly significant influence that led to considerable reflection was a book I received when I was in seventh grade. It was a best-selling novel titled *In His Steps: What Would Jesus Do?* written by Charles M. Sheldon, and first published in 1896. I initially read some of the early parts of the book, but lost interest since the illustrations seemed so far-fetched. Perhaps I didn't grasp that it was a story of fictional characters. I set it aside, but the question in the title kept haunting me. It came to mind in surprising ways during the next few years until it became part of my pattern of reflection on issues I was confronting. However, in subsequent years, when I went back to read the book more extensively, I realized I was applying it almost entirely to personal issues, while the book was applying it largely to social issues. It remains a recurrent part of my thinking, but I now apply it to both personal and social issues.

BECOMING PART OF A PARTICULAR NEIGHBORHOOD (5)

After moving back to 56th Street, I was old enough to explore the streets close to my new apartment in much greater detail than I could as a preschooler. Six years had passed, which meant I was at a different level of maturity, and the development of the very street where I lived had been modified. The huge lot almost directly across the street from where I was born had new townhomes lining that section of the block. Vacant land was almost nonexistent in this and several streets nearby. This meant there was no more playing in the dirt and bushes during the day; no more running through those lots and backyards at night.

Eighth Avenue had developed more fully in this neighborhood, and offered all kinds of interesting stores. Arne Bergman, who researched this area for almost twenty years, told me about his work when I visited Brooklyn on May 17, 2018, and spoke at the celebration of this important festival. He offered me a copy of his research when he heard I was thinking of writing a book about the colony in Brooklyn. (You can find a diagrammatic summary of the stores on Eighth Avenue from 54th to 60th Street in the third Appendix.) Some people referred to this section of Eighth Avenue as "the most Norwegian strip in Brooklyn." (Today, this avenue, and a substantial section of Sunset Park, is home to a vibrant Chinese community.)

The activities in which I was most engaged after school, and on weekends—besides studying—were all sorts of games. Many of them took place in the streets close to where I lived. Those that were most enjoyable during my junior high and senior high years were stickball, basketball (indoor and outdoor), skiing, ice skating, and swimming in the ocean (Coney Island), or in a pool (Sunset Park, St. George Hotel, YMCA). Others included softball, roller skating (indoor and outdoor), roller hockey, street games such as stoop ball, buck/buck, tag and hide/seek after dark, and of course, bicycling all over New York City—and beyond!

For stickball, all we really needed was a Spauldeen, a stick, and a piece of chalk. Practically every youth in Brooklyn played with, or knew about, the Spauldeen. The most common way to play took place on a one-way street, where two teams competed, using a modified version of baseball. One sewer cover in the middle of the street was home plate, and chalk drawings indicated the three bases. Some team members took positions at each base, while others scattered throughout the field of play. Batters were out when players caught a fly ball, threw a ground ball to a player at first base before the runner got there, or tagged a runner with the ball.

We didn't use pitchers or catchers when we played in the street. A batter got up and hit the ball by himself, either by bouncing the ball and hitting it after one or two bounces, or by tossing the ball in the air, and hitting it before it bounced on the ground.

One or more players from the team at bat watched for cars, and sometimes yelled "car," or stopped them if a runner was in motion. *Did drivers of cars toot their horns?* Of course! *Did they yell and sometimes swear at players who were in the paths of cars?* Sure! *Did those sounds affect the players?* No, not usually! *Did any player get hurt?* Not seriously! Drivers seemed to know they shared the streets with the players—or so we assumed. *Did the Spauldeen ever hit a pedestrian, or break a window?* Not very often.

Those at bat tried to let vehicles go through, and waited for elderly persons or small children to pass. *Did residents, or people walking on the sidewalks, get upset?* Not very often, because we were remarkably friendly. *Did people stop to watch us play?* Frequently, even cheering when they liked what they saw. *Did we carefully choose where we would play?* Certainly, most often on a side street with a limited number of parked cars, but occasionally on Ninth Avenue, when the traffic was light, since it was a two-way, wider street.

Sometimes I was at the edge of juvenile acts that were mischievous, but I most often limited myself to observing, or participating from a distance. I saw guys jump over the turnstiles at the subway stations without paying a fare; caught sight of guys putting a bag of excrement on a porch, lighting it with fire from lighter fluid, and then waiting for the person answering the bell to come and stamp it out; looked through the large, front glass windows of the tavern around the corner, when one of the guys slid a water-filled balloon down the long counter to see how many glasses he could knock off; observed some of the guys lifting the trolley pole of a streetcar off the wire so it couldn't move; then watched the conductor come out, look around, and put it back in place; joined others in throwing snowballs through open windows of moving cars and trucks after a storm. Were any of these actions dangerous to the recipients? We never thought about that. We only celebrated that we never got caught!

In addition to playing games after school, I worked to earn spending money even in my grade school years. I shoveled snow for neighbors, carried out groceries at the supermarket, and shined shoes at the street corner.

My new neighborhood had a Jewish delicatessen around the corner of 56th and Fort Hamilton Parkway. I stopped by for a get-acquainted visit, and was offered a job. Since I was only 12 years old, I had to get working papers signed by my parents. My responsibility was initially limited to delivering groceries, though it developed over the years to other areas. The name of the store was *Teitelbaum's,* since it was the last name of the owners.

The push cart they gave me to use was chained outside to a pole. It was the noisiest cart imaginable. My mother would often tell others, "You can hear it coming from a half a block away." It had three rusted steel wheels without any rubber between them and the concrete sidewalk. The two on the sides—outside the open, wooden box—were 42 inches high; the third in the front, under the box, was about 18 inches high. It could accommodate 6 to 8 large boxes of food.

I continued to work there through my years in junior and

senior high, beginning with 5¢ for each delivery—the amount an individual paid for a subway ride to Manhattan, or a ferry ride to Staten Island—plus a tip that was always more than a nickel, sometimes a lot more. I soon advanced to considerable increases in wages, carrying out responsibilities such as unpacking shipments, organizing shelves and cases, waiting on customers, and so forth. I ended up tasting so many Jewish foods that—looking back—I sometimes say *I ate my way into Judaism.* I learned about its faith and its applications to everyday life. In the process, I learned words in Yiddish, including the difference between a *schlemiel* and a *schlimazel.*

I left that position when I graduated from high school in 1955 and accepted full-time summer employment in a huge department store undergoing a major renovation. Thanks to my father who was not only a master carpenter there, but also the union steward, I became a Carpenter's Apprentice, a position a person could hold for up to six months in order to determine if he had the requisite skills to become a union carpenter. I earned union wages at high NYC rates, for those three months. My last weekly pay check was $126 in 1955, equivalent to $1,229 in 2021 (according to dollartimes.com).

I also heard, and sometimes learned—even unknowingly—many words and phrases with strictly Brooklyn pronunciations: *How ya doin? Yous tawkin to me? Whaddaya gonna do? Ya wanna bet? Jaeat yet? Ya gotta be kidden me. Not fer nuttin. Dem, dat, dowes, deese. Tirty tre. Whatchamacallit. Longuyland. Fughedaboudit!*

With the use of my bicycle and the access to buses and subways, I could travel throughout the entire city. I loved it! I felt so free. I could to go anywhere I wanted—without any restrictions unless I placed them on myself. However, I never went far away without a companion. That was an agreement I had with my parents and it turned out to be a wise practice in many situations, such as finding my way in new and strange places. I had someone with me to discuss where we were, where we wanted to go, and how we'd get there. We always found our way—eventually. We thoroughly enjoyed finding new places, even if we weren't sure where we were. That became so much fun that we sometimes got lost on purpose, whether we were riding on bicycles, buses, or subways. We were never afraid, because we never got lost to the extent that we couldn't figure out a way to reach our destination.

Transportation to the whole city (as I knew it) made me feel like it was my city. It's hard to describe the sense of ownership and freedom! I felt so much at home in my small, safe, and secure colony! But I learned some years later that I only related to a very small part of the city!

DISCOVERING INCREASED FREEDOM IN THE SECOND COLONY (6)

My parents loved spending time in Connecticut, especially in the summer. So did I, though I was beginning to wonder what was going on in Brooklyn during those months in my junior high years. To help me stay in touch with some of my close friends, my parents occasionally agreed to take me down to Brooklyn for a weekday visit, or bring those friends to Connecticut for a weekend. I particularly remember one Friday evening when my father drove up the hill to our cabin, got out of the car to greet my mother and me, and—all at once—Kenn, one of my closest friends, jumped out from the back seat. My father had made the arrangement to bring him to our cabin for the weekend. What a thoughtful dad!

When I heard news about what was happening with friends in Brooklyn, I was torn between going back there and staying where I was. I wanted to do both! After talking with my parents, and their reminding me it would only be a few weeks and I would be spending the whole school year there, I agreed to remain in Connecticut—particularly since that was the expectation we had set before the summer started.

As I reflected on all the good times we were having during those junior high summers at our cabin, my recollection turned to the fun we had at the lake. My sister, Elsie, and I, along with our next-door friends, Ruthie and Arthur, went swimming at a location known as the *dock*—eight bright yellow steel girders, heading out from shore for a distance of 15 feet. No one knew why there was no deck on top, but we guessed the state might have run out of money, or the water was not quite deep enough for diving off the end (which we all did anyway). Though it was on public land, it was outside the boundary of the state park, was less crowded, had no lifeguards, and no regulations. At least that was our assumption.

One day when the mothers of our two families were visiting on shore, the four of us started swimming toward the distant shore—at least a quarter of a mile away. When we were farther out than we had ever gone before, our mothers stood up, waved their arms, and repeatedly hollered, "Come back! Don't go any farther!" We saw them, heard them, and snickered as we treaded water, looked toward both shores, realized we were about halfway across, and that it was no further to swim to the other side than to return.

One of us blurted out, "Let's try it!" And we continued swimming or floating on our backs and kicking our feet. We were not good swimmers, but we had the courage and guts to make it! We understood that we had to keep going, once we started in that direction. Finally, when we could touch bottom on the other shore, the four of us stood up, faced our mothers, and waved, and hollered! Then, after resting for quite some time, we started back, and eventually made it. Were we scolded? Of course, though it soon dissipated when we shared the confidence and pride we felt in having reached the other side of the lake.

Occasionally, I would go fishing at the lake from one of the many piers, but usually only caught small fish I had to toss back. On one occasion, Clifford, my friend from church, came up from Brooklyn. We went fishing off one of the piers where we could easily look into the water. We had a can filled with night crawlers. After baiting our hooks and tossing in our lines, we both caught small sunfish fairly quickly. Seeing a number of larger fish in the area, we were eager to continue as soon as we could. We put on fresh worms and, as we were ready to put our lines in the water, Clifford yelled, "Oh, no!" I turned, and saw him looking so dejected. He pointed to numerous fish, especially the big ones, feasting on the worms from the can he had just kicked into the water. Incensed, he picked up one of the fish we had just caught, took a bite out of it, held it up, and said, "This is the only bait we have." We both laughed and decided to just watch the fish having a feast!

We also took a lot of hikes on paths into the woods, right up from our house. Other times we went with several families, driving cars to a trail head, and walking from there. A favorite was the path to the *Lookout,* from which we could view Candlewood Lake for miles in each direction. It was a long and arduous hike, but the view was well worth the climb. We finally reached a gray, weathered deck, and remained there for over an hour, eating our lunches, taking pictures, and telling stories. On our way down, we took a path different than the one on the way up, one that included a descent on rustic ladders through a series of huge boulders. It was so much fun. We could hardly wait for the next time!

We played a variety of indoor games such as Rook, Monopoly, or Parcheesi in late afternoons or evenings, sometimes with visiting neighbors or friends from Brooklyn. We also played games as a family on Sunday afternoons, especially when it was raining. On such a day, a severe storm arose, with teeming rain, howling winds, intense lightning, and deafening thunder. My mother, Elsie, and I stopped playing, looked out the window next to the game table, and watched the trees swaying wildly. My father, who had been relaxing in his big chair, got up and joined us in looking out the large, double window. Then a huge flash almost blinded us; everything went blank; a sound louder than any I had ever heard came crashing down as if it was a bomb going off inside our cabin. No one moved, or made a sound. We were momentarily stunned and terrified!

Then my father broke the silence and spoke in a firm voice, "I think we were just struck by lightning." And, at that moment my mother noticed that the huge oak tree less than a hundred feet from the window where we were siting, was split from top to bottom. We all looked out and saw the tree. My father spoke again, "That was really a close call," he said, "but I don't think it touched the house. I'll go outside and check." Although it was still lightly raining, we all got up, put on our jackets, went out to inspect the damage and talk about the cleanup that would be needed.

We also played outside games when the weather was favorable. Badminton was the most popular. One of the key reasons for this was the court that Mr. Olsen had built on the lower level of his hillside property on the other side—across the brook from our property. The ground, which was precisely leveled, was covered with a type of compacted soil that was periodically soaked with oil to keep it firm. The accurately measured boundary lines had steel rods painted white at the tips that easily could be seen without sticking up above the ground. Lines with small indentations were made in the ground, between the markers, for white lime—though that was a serious problem when it rained.

The following spring, Mr. Olsen surprised us as we came to play on the court. Instead of white lime between the markers, he surprised us with concrete lines, about two inches wide, four inches deep, and even with the ground. In each section of concrete he had inserted a piece of pipe to keep them firm and straight. They worked well during the summer season. But when frost was ready to enter the ground, he had to dig them up, clean and store them in the garage for the next season. He did reinstall them the following spring, but let all of us know it would not continue the following year; it was too much work!

Almost every Norwegian living in the neighborhood during the summer played badminton—children, youth, and adults. On Sunday afternoons, and on holidays, informal tournaments were organized according to ability, rather than age. I practiced very diligently with other youth so I could hold my own with the adults. I soon bought my own racquet and press, and professional shuttlecocks—the expensive ones with real feathers. I became the singles champion of the youth, and not long after, of the adults. I enjoyed playing those games, but I also enjoyed watching others play, especially the adults. Best of all was the playing in doubles, and the occasions when we were victorious! Did I love to win? I'll let you decide!

Another highlight for many of us each summer were the campfires. They took place at various homes, often with several additional family members and friends. However, not all homes could host a large gathering and a blazing fire. At our house, we had a special area for such an event, a considerable distance down the hill from our cabin, which meant carrying food, utensils, musical instruments, lanterns, serving tables, and chairs. In addition to eating, roasting marshmallows, and telling stories, we sang a variety of songs. I sometimes accompanied the group, or individuals singing solos, with my guitar. A favorite for all of us, but particularly the adults, was the Norwegian National Anthem:

Ja, vi elsker dette landet	Yes, we love this country
Som det stiger frem,	as it rises forth,
Furet, værbitt over vannet	Rugged, weathered over the water,
Med do tusen hjem.	with the thousand homes.
Elsker, Elsker det og tenker	Loving it, loving it, and thinking
På vår far og mor,	of our father and mother,
Og den saganatt som senker	And the saga night that lowers
Drømme på vår jord.	dreams upon our earth.

The word "saga" in this first verse refers to a heroic achievement, especially a medieval narrative in Old Norse.

The second verse (actually the seventh in the original version) begins with the opening line, *Norske mann, i hus og hytte, takk din store Gud!* ("Norwegian man in house and cabin, thank your strong God!")—an interesting reference to a house and a cabin, precisely what my father (and, of course, mother) had chosen to inhabit, though the house was actually an apartment in Brooklyn. Other families present also had a "house" and a "cabin."

During the late 1940s electricity was brought to our property, making cabin living much more enjoyable. Lights meant oil lamps didn't need to be filled; an electric stove didn't need flames from a kerosene container; a refrigerator didn't need large blocks of ice. Darkness outside the house gave way to light for visitors, as well as family members finding their way to the outhouse. It was such a dramatic change—such an enjoyable development!

Soon thereafter, an artesian well was drilled—over 300 feet in depth, through solid ledge—a project that took months of time, and cost a substantial amount of money. It was not only drilling at a very slow pace, but then installing a pipe most of the way down, and the equipment to bring the water up. But that was only the beginning. The water had to be brought into the house, but only after pipes had been installed. When it was all finally completed—-a few years later—we celebrated once again.

During these and subsequent years, my father was busy on Saturdays and vacation days to complete the interior of the house. In the kitchen, he built all the cabinets from ¾ inch knotty pine, and laid the linoleum floor with a contrasting border around the edges. In the living room, he laid a solid plank oak floor of 5-, 7-, and 9-inch widths. But he didn't stop there; he chiseled what he called *butterflies* at the edges of selected planks in such a way that half of the angled 1 x 2.5-inch piece of dark walnut was cut into each of the planks. In addition, he drilled two 0.75-inch round holes, into which he inserted round, dark walnut pieces, near the end of each plank, where it butted up against another plank. And, then, he had a professional come and sand the entire floor, prior to adding a protective matte finish.

The way the floor looked at the end of the process was so astounding that he covered it with a light woven carpet, so everyday walking would not mark it. When company came, he pulled a corner back to reveal what he had accomplished. It was a work of art, as were many other aspects in our house. I have met other fine master carpenters in my life, but none finer than my father!

LEARNING IN JUNIOR HIGH SCHOOL – PERSHING 220 (7)

Moving to a new apartment in the summer of 1950 meant a change of school, not only because the location was different, but also because the grade was a new educational level. That combination of circumstances made it more challenging, though more meaningful, since it was a return to a neighborhood that was familiar and desirable.

The new school, Pershing Junior High School, located at 4812 Ninth Avenue, took up the entire block from 48th to 49th Streets. It included grades 7 through 9 when I attended; now it's a middle school, open to grades 6 through 8. The ethnicity of the student body when I went there was largely European, particularly Italian and Eastern European, though Norwegian, Finish, Irish, and Polish students were also present in noticeable numbers. That makeup has changed dramatically over the years. Now the population is approximately 50% Asian, 42% Latinx, 6% White, and 2% African American.

The name of the class I entered was *7-8 Special 1.* (There was also a *7-8 Special 2.)* This meant that those of us in it—14 boys and 14 girls—would engage in seventh grade work for the first two-thirds of the year, and the first half of eighth grade work for the last one-third. It may sound confusing, but was carried out smoothly. The difficulty most of us in the class had was working through our educational identity. This was even more pronounced for other students who weren't sure what our category was. Toward the end of the year, we thought of ourselves as eighth graders. In the following academic year, when we were in *8-9 Special 1,* we did eighth grade work for the first third of the year, and ninth for the remainder. We became known as *9 Special 1* as the year moved on. Everyone in the school accepted us as ninth graders. That felt really good!

The use of the word *special* brought about a variety of comments, often in a derogatory manner by those not in the class. But those of us in our class didn't feel we were better than other students, and we tried our best not to act as though we were special. Over time, that issue subsided as we formed close friendships outside of our class—an easy approach for me since my meaningful relationships were largely outside class identities. Occasionally I was ribbed by those in my peer group, but always with a sense of fun.

Being elected to *Arista,* the Honor Society for students, helped my sense of belonging with other students, many of whom were Italians (often attending Roman Catholic churches) and Eastern Europeans (almost always Jewish, both culturally and religiously). Those relationships broadened my perspective as I listened and tried to understand their points if view. Discussions sometimes involved issues raised in my class, since a large number of those students were also in the Honor Society.

At home, it was interesting to connect with my parents regarding what was taking place at school. They wanted to know what I was learning since they had not been able to pursue their education beyond grade school. In addition, my mother loved to hear stories about school. On the evening of my first day in junior high, after we had finished eating dinner, Elsie went to her room to study for her classes, and my father moved into the living room to sit in his favorite chair.

My mother, who remained with me in the kitchen, smiled as she asked me a question: "Are there any cute girls in your class?" I immediately thought of a particular girl, sitting in front of me, one row over.

"Oh yes, she sits near me," I responded. "She has a beautiful smile, and is so pretty!"

"What's her name?"

"Myra Moskowitz," I responded.

My father, sitting on the other side of the archway, said: "Doesn't sound Norwegian to me." My mother and I laughed.

"She's really cute," I said as I looked around the archway at my father and saw him smiling.

When I reached ninth grade, I became a member of the Color Guard, a particularly meaningful activity to me. It consisted of 42 students—boys and girls dressed in school colors of navy-blue slacks and skirts, and white shirts and blouses—who marched and carried five flags to the beat of a drum at highly honorable events at school. The main reason it meant a lot to me was connected to the American flag that my parents proudly displayed at the top of the flag pole on the lawn outside their cabin in Connecticut, honoring their citizenship in the United States. And not only that, but also the Norwegian flag hanging just beneath it, honoring the land of their birth. It was a patriotic time in the history of our country!

Although Will Herberg's book, *Protestant, Catholic, Jew: An Essay in American Religious Sociology* was not published until 1955, and I didn't read it until some years later, I share its primary thesis here. It represents precisely what my experience was in junior high, and the years that followed. He argued that America had become a three-religion country. The dominance of Protestantism was waning; the places of Catholicism and Judaism were on the rise. However, he was criticized for being too simplistic. Religion in America was actually becoming a more complex group of entities. Yet for me, as a Protestant in the early 1950s, the awareness of a three-religion nation was real. I had numerous friends in school who were Protestants, Catholics, and Jews.

Our graduating class of 1952 had 468 students—280 boys and 188 girls, out of a total school enrollment of approximately 1,400 students. Many of these graduates, including most of those who were Norwegian in heritage, went to Fort Hamilton High School. The classes I took at Pershing Junior High during the two years I was there prepared me remarkably well for the next three years. I entered high school with clarity regarding my class identity. I was a sophomore like any other entering student. It was such a relief!

ENGAGING IN ACTIVITIES BEYOND SCHOOL (8)

During my junior high years, and continuing through my senior high years, I traveled within and beyond the colony. One of the ways I did that was riding my bicycle from my home to other places close to where I lived. However, that boundary expanded rapidly, until it included all five boroughs and locations farther away. I went exploring all over the city with one or more of my friends from the colony, never thinking we might have a flat tire (though I did carry some patches and goo in a small bag under the seat).

My friends and I had different kinds of bikes. I still had my first bike, the one with balloon tires, though it was no longer loaded with accessories such as two headlights and taillights, white-wall tires, luggage carrier with double saddle bags, horn encased in a lengthy metal holder, leather seat encased in a chrome setting—all decorated in fancy colors and designs. No, the bicycle that I had put together to show off its appearance, changed from being a *maximalist* to a *minimalist.* I discarded the fenders, luggage rack, and saddle bags. Replacements included a loud, but small, ringing bell; a plain, comfortable seat; effective reflectors front and rear; and a bright blue paint job. It was a different bike in a different world!

My mother could no longer track where I went, and didn't even try. She would only say phrases such as: "Don't go alone;"

or, "Don't go too far"—whatever that meant. She reminded me, "Don't get lost; but if you do, ask somebody for help"—a request I don't think we ever made. However, there were also words of encouragement: "Have a good time." Or, "Enjoy your ride."

Some of our favorite places to ride were in parks. A highly desirable one was Shore Road Park, a 58-acre elongated strip of land alongside that portion of the harbor known as The Narrows. The views of Staten Island, the Statue of Liberty, and the skyline of Manhattan were spectacular, especially on a moonlit night. So were the sights over the water, where the traffic of passenger ships, tugboats, freighters, tankers, ferries, power boats, and sailboats moved in different directions, revealing a myriad display of activities.

In some areas, green space was on the other side of the parkway that paralleled the bike path. Included in some of those spaces were athletic fields, especially those given over to baseball and softball. Park benches were located along this biking and walking trail, next to the wrought iron and stone wall fencing. Pedestrian bridges across the parkway also were plentiful, though parking areas for cars facing the harbor were few. According to common folklore, the spaces were used primarily by couples, especially in later evening hours, who could look through their windshields and watch *submarine races*, or *flounder fights*.

Other parks included Clove Lakes Parks—three of them located as a group on Staten Island. To reach the numerous bike trails scattered throughout the 193 acres of lush greenery, we first rode to the Staten Island Ferry, located at the waterfront and 69th Street in Brooklyn, then enjoyed the ferry ride across the harbor, and continued on the roads leading to the parks. At other times, we took the same ferry, but went on other roads to Wolfe's Pond, a beautiful and serene park of more than 300 acres, also located on Staten Island. It was such a treat to have these and other parks at such close proximity to our colony.

Bikes were our common mode of transportation to such locations. Had it been necessary to reach them by other means, we would have relied on one or more buses in Brooklyn—depending on the street on which we lived—followed by the ferry ride, the bus or buses to reach our destination, and then walking after we arrived. Added to these burdens would have been the need to get bus schedules, wait for the buses to arrive, and pay fares that could easily add up to a considerable amount.

Another primary mode of transportation was the NYC subway system. With a stop in the colony on Eighth Avenue and 62nd Street, it was the means to reaching the other three boroughs: Queens, Manhattan, and Bronx. Learning how to use them entailed simply getting on and taking a ride. Each car had a colored map on the wall, and each station had a name, scattered on the walls throughout the station. At first it seemed frightening, but the reassurance that was abundantly provided by my friends, meant you would never be by yourself—assuming you didn't start out alone. Like bike riding, the rule I followed that gave comfort to my parents, especially my mother, was "always go with a friend." That meant, if you get lost, at least you won't be alone. Did I get lost? Of course, dozens and dozens of times! It really didn't matter! I'd study the map on the wall; watch the sign at the next stop; and decide to stay on, or get off. If I couldn't decide, I'd simply stay on, study the map some more, confer with my friends, and answer these three questions: Where am I? Where do I want to go? How can I get there?

To complicate matters, I had to learn if I was on a local or an express subway, as well as whether or not a station was a local or express stop. And to add to the complexity, I had to learn whether the car I was on, or wanted to be on, was a part of the BMT, IRT, or IND system. And then the jackpot question: Do I need to make a change—or two, or even three—to get to the location I want to reach? It became clear to me that the best way to learn was to get on, start moving, make all sorts of decisions, and see what turns up! It was a puzzle waiting to be solved!

I eventually enjoyed it, though it was frustrating at first; however, it became a competition within myself, as well as with my friends. Did that open the whole world of NYC? It sure did! And the results of that process were enormous! I lost so much of my fear about the unknown, fear of going to places I had never been; fear of doing things I had never tried; fear of meeting people I had never met. I was also learning to trust my own judgment. And it felt very good!

We also played games on the subways. At one station in mid-town Manhattan was an escalator that went from one platform below street level, to another platform two levels farther down. The game was for one of the guys from our group, trying to show off—especially to the gals—deciding to run as rapidly as possible, up the down escalator, and reach the top before the next person got on. If successful, the guy faced the group to the applause of all. If someone got on the escalator before he reached the top—the most common result—he had to face his friends below and listen to the boos and hisses on his way down. Strangers watching sometimes cheered or booed with us.

Another event that must have been incredibly exciting—though I never learned the final result—was when Torvald, father of my friend, Ruthie, stopped by Sheepshead Bay on his way home from work. He and his family loved crabs. He bought a dozen—fresh from the bay and still alive—had them wrapped in enough newspaper and heavy string to get them home safely. But that evening the subway moved very slowly, and then came to a halt in a dimly lit tunnel. After fifteen or twenty minutes, he felt a couple of claws starting to protrude through the wet paper. He didn't think much about it but simply turned the package over and held it as carefully as he could. When the subway failed to move, he tried fixing the paper as several other claws began to poke through. Not able to figure out any solution, he slid the package under his seat, stood up, and after moving through a lot of people, reached the door to the next car, opened it, and left. What happened next? We never found out.

Other activities during these junior high years included roller skating all over the neighborhood in shoe skates with solid, ball-bearing wheels, sometimes while holding on to a horse-drawn milk wagon. Or, playing for one season on a brutal, neighborhood roller hockey team called *The Skulls,* on a Parks Department smoothly finished court with steel framed nets at each end. Or, sledding on city streets after new snow had fallen, hanging on to the bumpers of cars as they pulled away from a stop sign. Or, going on Boy Scout trips that included sleeping in outdoor lean-tos, regardless of the weather.

Although outdoor swimming was popular in warm months, indoor swimming was trendy in cold months. The place of choice was the saltwater, Olympic-sized pool at St. George Hotel, only a short subway ride from the colony. It had been restricted to people in show business, but it recently had been opened to the public, including its renowned swimming pool. We had to use their bathing suits, which were small and tight. I got mine, went into the locker room, and tried to pull it on, but I couldn't pull it all the way up. I went back to the attendant and asked for a larger size. He gave it to me, but said, "Remember, the bathing suit will get larger when it gets wet." I said I understood, but took the larger size.

I put that one on and it felt fine out of the water. I got to the pool, eased my way into the water, and became aware the suit had gotten bigger, but thought I'd pull it up if that was needed. A friend then came to the edge of the pool, pointed, and said, "I just dove in from that diving board. It's great when you see all the underwater lights." I climbed the ladder out of the pool, and followed him. He dove first; I followed. And then, right after I hit the water, I realized my suit had slid down to my knees. I was stunned, and hurriedly pulled up my suit. It had gotten so much larger! I got out of the pool and headed back to the attendant.

"Sir, may I have a smaller size?"

"Here's the one I gave you before," he said, smiling. "Just leave the other one in the locker room." As I walked down the hall to the locker room, I kept wondering to myself: *Who was in the pool next to me?*

GROWING UP: INTERNALIZING MY VALUES (9)

I began to develop my values in my preschool years. I developed them further in my grade school years. I internalized them increasingly in my junior high years. This ongoing process enabled them to become my own values.

My parents shared their values, not by talking about them, but by demonstrating them by the way they lived. Their understanding was rooted in Norwegian terminology that was not always easy to express in English. This meant they focused on doing what they believed was right—perhaps not clearly realizing what they were doing. They often used the word *right* without defining its meaning.

For my mother, speaking of something being *right* often was expressed from a negative perspective—something that was *not right.* It might be the way a dress she was trying on at the store didn't fit properly. She would simply say, "It's not right." Or, it might be something a person was doing that didn't receive her approval. She would say, "That's not right." I heard those words over and over again, throughout my years of growing up.

For my father, the approach was similar. When we were working on a project—often something we were building out of wood—he would say, "If you're going to do it, you might as well do it right." It might be measuring something twice to make sure it was the correct length, before cutting it. Or, taking the time to find the right screws to make sure they would hold properly. Or, not using the zinc-coated links to make the exterior connection when there were some that were right—the ones that were stainless steel.

I grew up with the understanding that many things in life were either right or wrong. I learned, even in my junior high and senior high years, that many situations in life were not clear cut. But I often thought about whether an action was right or not, and lived out of a script that sought to do what was right. It had become my moral framework, my primary criterion for making personal decisions, my basis for defining values.

Since my parents didn't articulate rules for my behavior, I lived primarily by values they had expressed. But I was at the age of reflecting on those values, and deciding on those to fully embrace (as I understood them at that time), and those to question, or even reject. The pattern I chose to follow—more by not resisting, than by intentional choosing—was to continue living by the values I had been shown, while at the same time, making them my own.

As a result, I hardly ever got into conflict with my parents. They didn't tell me what to do. They didn't give me rules to follow. They had shared boundaries with me in my earliest years on 56th Street ("Don't go in the street. Stay on the sidewalk between our apartment and the corner.") and in

Connecticut ("You can go anywhere, as long as you can see the house"). But when those didn't work, they shared values that would influence my behavior ("Don't go by yourself. Be careful. Be considerate of others.")

As I grew older, my parents didn't talk with me regarding what time I should be home. They would simply repeat the gist what they had said in earlier years, but expressing it in more positive terms. Instead of the negative connotation in the words "Don't stay out too late," they would say words in a more positive manner: "Have a good time." Or, in Norwegian *Ha det godt!* In this way, my mother and father would follow a pattern of not setting rules, but affirming values. At the time, I don't think they, or I, consciously realized the implications of what they were doing.

To what extent was this a result of my doing what pleased them? Or, was it that they didn't know much of what I was doing—primarily focusing on who I was with? There was a lot I didn't tell them in detail, and my mother and father almost never asked me for such details after I gave them an overall summary. They assumed I was a good boy, and generally didn't ask about specifics.

The decision to be a follower of Jesus that I made when I was six years old, coupled with the question in the title of the book *In His Steps: What Would Jesus Do?* led me to focus the basis of my values in the life of Jesus. Study of the Four Gospels in the New Testament increasingly became the foundation for my thoughts and actions. In the midst of my learning, I was drawn to the person of Jesus and the way he lived. And through a relationship with him as the risen Lord, and through my interaction with my friends in the colony, I kept reflecting on the question, *What Would Jesus Do?* As I did this, I attempted not only to think through my values, but to apply them in my daily life.

DEVELOPING TRUST IN MYSELF (10)

I experienced trust in my parents, and their trust in me, during my preschool years. I broadened this trust by reaching out to others in the colony, as they also placed their trust in me, in my grade school years. However, during my junior high years, my trust—just like my values—became internalized.

Riding my bicycle and traveling by subway, not only in Brooklyn, but in the entire city, gave me numerous opportunities to trust myself, though not always without some degree of fear. However, as successful responses to experiences gave me increasing confidence, my trust in myself deepened.

I learned to take risks, because I believed I not only *could* find a way to handle whatever emerged, but I *would*. As a result, risk-taking increased, though only after careful consideration of particular consequences as well as overall impact. This openness to new possibilities took place not only with transportation throughout the city, but also with activities that were new or different. Yet the application of my values to such experiences functioned as safeguards to inappropriate behavior.

As a result, I learned a great deal, though I increasingly became aware that my learning was largely from visual and auditory sources, not from information gleaned from books. As I've already shared, I didn't read much, in part because we had very few books in our home. My parents only read a weekly paper in Norwegian, the *Nordisk Tidende* (published in Brooklyn), and a daily paper in English, the *Daily News*. I did read the textbook assignments that my teachers gave, but generally not much beyond that—an approach that dramatically changed in my post high school education that led to earning four academic degrees, including a PhD.

I didn't realize the importance of my response to the visual and auditory learning that I experienced, particularly overcoming my fear about life outside the colony that I initially felt. The process of shedding the fear of getting lost that initially took place during my junior high years, carried on not only through my senior high years, but through my entire life. I am still reminded of my learning from the subway rides, particularly when I read statements such as the one I saw on a t-shirt while writing this part of the book: *GET LOST—It's a destination, not a reprimand!*

During my junior high years, I learned to trust myself, take risks, and do things on my own. At the same time, I also was in the process of learning the limitations and dangers of such an approach. I was part of a colony of wonderful Norwegian people in Brooklyn—approximately 62,000 of them—who were quite resourceful to me, often in ways far beyond what I realized. At the heart of these people were my peers—brothers and sisters from different mothers and fathers!

CHAPTER 4

SENIOR HIGH YEARS

(1952-55)

BELONGING TO A BROADER PEER COLONY (1)

I continued to live at 932 56th Street as in the prior two years. Had I spent 3 years in junior high, instead of 2, I would have lived in each of the 3 apartments during my period of "growing up" for 6 years. It was not only coincidental that I moved at times I changed schools, but fortunate in that the students in each school were unique to a particular location. I was in a central part of the Norwegian colony in my preschool years, at the edge of the colony in my grade school years, and back in the central part in my junior and senior high years. The contrast inherent in each of those moves contributed to my understanding of an inside and outside perspective toward the colony.

These changes in location, and the simultaneous changes in schools, were such privileges for me. They were very different for my sister, Elsie. She lived in our first apartment for 9 years, and attended grades 1 through 4 at P.S. 105. When we moved to 845 44th Street, she entered fifth grade in P.S. 169 and continued there through eighth grade. She moved to Bay Ridge High School in ninth grade—her third public school. These changes—circumstantially necessitated—were far more difficult for her than for me, though I didn't recognize her struggle and, at the same time, my privilege.

During my senior high years I realized some of the ways my broader group of peers were installing social trust in the colony, particularly in the area of athletics (though I would not have expressed it in those terms at the time). One of the ways took place when a group of guys got together to play "3 on 3" (a basketball expression for two groups of three competing against each other) at the outdoor playground of P.S. 105. Whoever brought the ball was automatically captain of one team, and chose two others to join him. Another guy volunteered to be captain of the second team, and chose two from the remaining group to join him.

When the guys played (on half of the full-sized court), and one team scored five baskets, they stopped, and whoever was next among those who were waiting to play, picked two others to join him as the new team. Sometimes the next team was three new persons; other times it was a combination of new and current players. When a new arrival showed up, he assumed last place and waited his time to choose a team. Turns were always respected; no one was left out; everyone got a chance to play, even when the new guy didn't play very well!

A similar spirit of inclusion took place on the softball field—most often at Shore Road Park, reached by bus, subway, or car. As a group of guys and gals (typical terminology in the 1950s) gathered, and there were enough for two teams, two captains emerged in a variety of ways, though not usually the two best players. It was common for a member of the group—sometimes a youth leader—to ask: "Who's willing to be a captain, who hasn't had a chance before?" After one person responded, the same question was asked again. If no one responded the second time, then some verbal interaction that led to a form of consensus surfaced, and the choosing of team members began. The attempt was for everyone who was interested to have an opportunity to be a captain.

We never discussed, but often practiced, social trust. As a result, guys and gals regularly experienced a sense of belonging. This was certainly true for me. The older ones were remarkably thoughtful, and regularly left room for the younger ones. It was like one big family, at least most of the time.

The experience of belonging, even in circles wider than my initial peer group, meant a lot to me. I was now a sophomore in high school, and didn't have to deal with the ambiguity of being in, or between, two grade levels as I did in junior high. In addition, I didn't have to deal with relating to two churches—Bethelship and 59th Street. I had been confirmed in one, and had become a member of the other. I didn't have to move to a new apartment just before starting a new school. My identity was clear, and I felt more secure!

My involvements in school, church, and neighborhood had not only become stabilized, but they gave me new relationships with a broader peer colony. I could now relate to others in age groups beyond my own—junior highs younger than me, and high school graduates older than me. As the 3 years in high school developed, I became enriched beyond my expectations and fulfilled in ways that increased my meaning and purpose for living.

I loved life, even with the struggles and disappointments that were part of it. I was increasingly confident that I could handle whatever might happen!

REDEFINING CONNECTIONS WITHIN AN EXTENDED FAMILY (2)

I grew up in a colony comprised of family and friends. With only a small immediate family, I found myself—either by circumstance or by choice—in a large family that was functional rather than biological. In addition, I related to others as friends rather than family; they were persons in the colony with whom I got acquainted, but with whom I didn't establish a close relationship.

My extended family at first emerged from relatives and close friends of my parents. However, my initial peer group rapidly became my functional brothers and sisters—having had only one biological sister and no biological brother. Their parents, and sometimes their siblings, became my functional aunts and uncles. Others at 59th Street Church, especially the basketball team known as the "Lutherans," also became a part of my functional family.

As soon as I was old enough to come out for the team in junior high, I started to play. However, it was not until I was in high school that I officially became a member of the team and received a uniform (shorts and a cream-colored tank top with my own number, and the name "Lutherans" emblazoned across it in a bright maroon color). I was neither one of the starting five, nor one of the first off the bench; but I did play in every game. I belonged to a group of guys—some of whom were like brothers to me. Best of all, we individually bought reversible jackets that were at least equal to the varsity letterman jackets of the Fort Hamilton High School team.

The first day I wore the jacket into my high school, I was incredibly proud of belonging to the "Lutherans," especially when students I passed in the hallways, asked about the team, or made complimentary statements about the jacket! Did I turn it inside out to show the bright maroon satin cloth, with lettering in a sharply contrasting cream color? Certainly! Was I smiling broadly as I responded to comments from the students? Of course! I knew I belonged, and felt the joy from deep within!

I was also a part of other groups that I would include

in my extended family. At school it was Trinity Club, a student-led organization that met once a month in the large music room known as Recital Hall. It brought together more than 100 students who were interested in, or committed to, the Christian faith, mostly from Protestant churches—Baptist, Lutheran, Methodist, Pentecostal, Presbyterian—though some also from Catholic churches. At our meetings we sang hymns and choruses, accompanied by a piano, and occasionally other instruments. A guest youth leader often shared the meditation, though sometimes a student would speak. I had the privilege of serving as president my senior year. Many in the club were like brothers and sisters to me.

Youth organizations were also part of my extended family. One of those was Hi-BA, rarely called by its full name (High School Born-Againers), not only because it was cumbersome to pronounce, but because some youth felt it was an understanding of the Christian faith that did not adequately represent their beliefs. But the activities they led, particularly the overnight retreats, were highly successful—especially those that were ski trips to Pennsylvania and Vermont (the two I attended).

The trip to the Pocono Mountains in Pennsylvania took place in the winter of my sophomore year. To avoid paying a rental fee, I brought with me a pair of wooden skis from Norway that I had borrowed from *Oncle Olaf* and *Tante Dagny*. I tried them on before leaving in order to adjust the bindings—large coiled springs that were tightly clamped to the back of the combat boots I had purchased at the Army and Navy store on Eighth Avenue. I was excited to have the skis with me since they were authentically Norwegian. Little did I know that they were quite thick and heavy, compared to the slender, light-weight skis available for rent. Furthermore, the binders held the skis firmly to the boots, regardless of falls that would take place. I also brought a pair of bamboo ski poles I had borrowed. I was dressed in jeans and my father's old blue jacket, but I had Norwegian knitted gloves and hat. I thought I would be ready for a great time of skiing! But there was one thing missing: I didn't know how to ski.

After getting on my gear, I saw my friend, Rolf, and my favorite youth group leader, Don, coming across the beautiful, new fallen snow. They were both experienced skiers, easily the best in our group of 30 to 40 guys and gals. Don began the conversation by asking, "Adolf, earlier you said you didn't know how to ski, and that you wanted to learn."

"Yes, that's what I want," I replied.

"You'll have to decide whether you want to learn the correct moves—one at a time—and become a good skier, using proper form. That'll take some time," said Rolf. "Or, you can learn to overcome your fear, stay up on your skis most of the time, and fall without getting hurt—all in one day!"

"I think I'll go with the second option. What do I have to do?"

"You'll have to practice falling all day. Yes—all day—falling as soon as you get moving; then skiing a little faster, and falling again; then skiing down a hill, going still faster, and falling again. One of us will stay with you for your first few falls, and show you how to place your weight, and what to do with your poles when you fall. We'll also show you how to use the rope tow to get back up the hill."

I didn't realize the pain of falling—over and over again. But I took some breaks, watched others ski, and stopped for lunch. I didn't want to go back out on the hills after eating and sitting by the fire talking with friends, but Don came along and said to all of us, "Okay, it's time to get skiing again. If you need some help, come talk with me." As he started out the door, he said to me, "Hang in there, Adolf; tomorrow I'll share more; but today, it's your job to fall, go faster, and fall again."

I did precisely that, skiing faster and faster, and learning how to fall, better and better—a total of somewhere between 50 and 60 times. That evening, and the next morning, I was really sore, but I had learned to go down steeper and steeper slopes without getting hurt. Skiing had become ingrained in me!

The following winter our group went skiing at Big Bromley in Vermont. I wore the same ski outfit, brought the same gear and had a fantastic experience. This time I learned to turn by using a snow plow methodology. It gave me much more control of where I was going, though my form was strangely awkward. The first day there, after I had tried the rope tows a couple of times, I saw Rolf and Don heading toward the main J-Bar lift that went up the center of the highest hill at the resort. I waved to them, and they paused until I reached them. They indicated where they were going, and I asked if I might go with them. They were hesitant, but finally agreed to show me how to get on and off the lift. They also told me about a trail I could ski down if I decided not to go down the steep hill.

We went up on the lift, but as we were getting off, I fell. Rolf helped me get up, and we moved to a flat area surrounding the top of the hill, where we could look down. I was petrified! The hill was so steep I couldn't see the bottom! Don said to Rolf, "I'll meet you at the bottom," and pushed off. Rolf followed, and I was left alone. Having more guts than brains at that moment, I started to go down without fully realizing what was happening. I momentarily remembered Rolf had told me when we were skiing in the Poconos, "If you feel like you're getting out of control, FALL! And that's exactly what I did. I slid for what seemed like the length of a football field, and finally came to a stop—covered with a lot of snow, fairly confident I hadn't gotten hurt, skis still attached to my boots, and my poles intact.

As the thought—*I did it*—was flashing in my mind, I heard a man's voice say to me, "Don't move! We're the ski patrol. We'll get you down." I looked at him, turned my body toward him, and saw the stretcher they were starting to put next to me.

"I'm okay. I can get down by myself," I said to the two men who were standing over me.

One of the men looked at me and asked, "What are you doing up here? You shouldn't be on this trail." He examined my combat boots and said, "You're not even wearing ski boots!" Scrutinizing my skis, he added, "You have spring clamps holding your skis on—attachments skiers no longer use. They're too dangerous. They prevent separation of the skis from the boots!"

I don't remember my response. I just got up, brushed off the snow, and angled down the rest of the hill, hoping I wouldn't have to fall before I got to the bottom. I made it, all the while thinking about my accomplishment, and looking forward to telling Rolf, Don, and my extended family that I skied down the steepest hill at Big Bromley!

DEEPENING RELATIONSHIPS WITH FRIENDS (3)

Many types of relationships emerged within the colony. Most common for me were those that involved my peers, both in individual and group settings. Sometimes it was primarily one guy; other times one gal. But in either circumstance, the group was also a part of it.

I met Rolf, my best friend of all, at 59th Street Church. He had attended a different grade school and junior high, and was enrolled at Brooklyn Technical High School—restricted to boys who had passed demanding entrance requirements. He was a year ahead of me, but that didn't seem to be a concern. What mattered was that both of us sang and played the guitar.

And it didn't take long before we were singing and playing duets together in youth meetings in our church as well as other places. We became known as the *Rolf-a-Dolf Duo,* though that name was not widely known.

I was pleasantly surprised to learn that Rolf was born in Flekkefjord, Norway—the birthplace of my father—and had come to the United States when he was two years old. His older sister, Oddfrid, was married to Art Tokle, who became America's national champion in ski jumping in 1951 and 1953, and competed in the Winter Olympics in Squaw Valley in 1960. No wonder Rolf was an excellent skier, as well as my ski instructor at the Poconos and Big Bromley. Rolf was also an accomplished guitar player, able to play interludes in the songs we sang, while I strummed chords—eventually any chord in any key—to accompany him. With my voice reaching a higher pitch than his, I usually harmonized the songs to the melodies he was singing. The result was a blending of voices and guitars that received rave reviews wherever we sang and played.

We were both so keenly interested in unusual musical sounds that we purchased electric attachments that enabled us to play with the assistance of an amplifier and its adjustable tremolo effects. We continued to learn new and intriguing sounds from books, sheet music, and the performances of other singers.

One evening, as the two of us were walking on the boardwalk at Coney Island, we heard guitar music coming from a crowded bar. We stopped and looked inside, through the large side doors that were open, since we were too young to enter. A man we called "the bouncer" came over and started to tell us to move. We told him we just wanted to watch the chords the singer was using. "Okay," he said, "but only if you don't stay too long, and don't block patrons from getting in or going out."

Rolf and I watched closely, and then he spoke to me in a

hushed voice: "Adolf, did you see that? He used a ninth rather than a seventh chord as the transition to the dominant chord. Let's try that as soon as we get home."

When we sang and played together, several songs became favorites. One that our audiences requested more than any other was "Tenderly He Watches Over You." It begins with a powerful affirmation: *Tenderly He watches over you, every step, every mile of the day.* We often invited whomever was present to join us in a repetition of the refrain—sometimes the entire song. They loved to sing it, and we loved to hear them!

Barbara, who played the piano with exquisite skill, sometimes joined us with her accordion (that she called her *Stomach Steinway*) for accompaniment and interludes, and with her voice as another harmonic addition. At other times, Govie joined us with his melodious voice, his guitar, or more frequently, his steel guitar. We chose the name *Hagola Valley Boys*: *Ha* for Hansen, *go* for Govertsen, and *la* for Larsen.

Some of the secular musical selections Rolf and I sang were in a western style. Eddie Arnold and Hank Snow were two of Rolf's favorites. On occasions when we performed that type of music, we wore pastel shirts, embroidered in colorful threads on the collars and sleeves, and four pearl buttons on each of the cuffs. We even had cowboy boots and hats to match. And if that wasn't enough, we both learned to yodel individually, and sometimes interspersed those sounds in a couple of our selections!

Other close friends included the gals I dated. Sometimes this was done in group settings Where we stayed together, such as the times we went to Jahn's Ice Cream Parlor—a short car ride provided by older friends. Who sat next to whom, and who paid for whom, was always an interesting game, especially when someone ordered *The Kitchen Sink* (a taste of almost all flavors of ice cream, syrups, and fruit). The person who devoured it had to stand and recite the words: "I made a pig of myself at Jahn's Ice Cream Parlor." Every time we went someone in our group ordered it, or had it ordered for them.

At other group settings such as ice skating, a guy would ask a gal to skate with him for a short or long part of the evening. Or, when a group of us went on a five-cent ferry ride across the harbor to Staten Island and back (sometimes for the same nickel if you secretly didn't get off), two of us would sometimes separate from the group and spend time together in the moonlight. Likewise, when a group of us went on two ferry rides, first to Staten Island, and then on a ten-cent ride to Manhattan, and back. Such connecting with a group, as well as an individual gal, occurred during numerous other activities, at a variety of locations scattered all over Brooklyn and the other four boroughs.

However, there were also individual dates that took place separate from any group. When I wanted to go see the rodeo at Madison Square Garden, I asked Lita if she wanted to go. She readily accepted. When the evening came around, I went to pick her up at her upstairs apartment (where we had previously spent time sitting on her porch nestled under some large trees). I greeted her parents, whom I had already met, visited for a short time, and then, as we were about to leave, her father asked, "Do you have enough money to bring Lita back?" I smiled and assured him I did. We left, walked to the subway station, and headed for Manhattan.

On many other occasions, I asked a gal to go on a date. Sometimes it was for a walk with a stopover at a particular location. A memorable one was when Kirsten and I walked a short distance from her house, across the 92nd Street walking bridge over the Belt Parkway to the path along The Narrows waterfront. We stopped and sat on a bench overlooking the water. I had my arm around her shoulder as we gazed at the stars and listened to the waves overlapping the rocks at the shoreline.

All of a sudden, we heard the sound of voices and shoes running behind us. Then, almost immediately, three guys, appeared out of the darkness into the dim light from a light post—about fifteen feet to the side of us. They stopped momentarily, looked us over, mumbled some words to each other, and then took off down the path along the shoreline. We didn't speak a word to each other until they were out of sight. Were we frightened? We certainly were. Our hearts were racing. We asked each other: Who were they? Where did they come from? What were they doing? Why did they stop? Why didn't they say anything to us? Were they out to rob us? Were they there to molest us? Or, were they out for some late evening jogging—a possibility we didn't even consider until some hours later.

We talked quietly with each other, sat motionless, watched and listened to determine if they were coming back. After relaxing a bit, and letting our hearts quiet down, we headed toward the walking bridge. We shared ideas that were as humorous as we could make them. Did they see my physique and realize they couldn't easily take me down, since there were only three of them? Or, did they realize Kirsten could let out a loud shriek that would bring others to our rescue? And so the conversation continued until we reached her house. *Did she tell her parents?* Are you kidding! *Did I tell my parents?* Are you serious! *Did we tell some of our friends?* Of course we did! And they added to our narrative of why they left us alone, with thoughts that were hilarious!

An additional memory was inviting Kirsten to go with me to the Junior Gala, a festive occasion sponsored by a group of churches. It took place at a fancy hotel in midtown Manhattan and celebrated the end of the junior year in high school. I inquired whether she wanted to go in formal attire. She was quick to indicate she would love to go in that style—even though that was only suggested, not required. I made plans to rent a tuxedo, never having done that before. Her parents offered to purchase a fancy cocktail-length gown for her. I also contacted my friend Roy, and asked if he would share the cost of renting a limo to take the four of us to the hotel. He concurred and I made the arrangement to rent a stretch limousine Cadillac.

When the Friday in late May arrived, I took the city bus to Kirsten's home, rang the bell while holding a fancy packaged orchid corsage in my hand, and greeted her mother at the door. As I entered, Kirsten's father welcomed me with a broad smile and a handshake. Then, my date walked into the room, wearing a light blue, formal gown—looking more gorgeous than I had ever seen her. As she went with her mother to put on the corsage, I told her father a limo was coming to pick us up. He smiled and said, "I'll watch for it through the front windows."

It wasn't long before a shiny black Cadillac, with fishtails at the rear, pulled up. As Kristen and I went out, we saw several neighborhood children gathering around the car. When we walked toward it, the children asked if we were going to a wedding. We smiled, but didn't respond. We said goodbye to Kirsten's parents, and headed on to pick up Roy and his date more than a mile away. As we drove, I felt so important, as people waved to us at stop signs and traffic lights. Then we continued the lengthy ride to the hotel, stopped at the front entrance, and were greeted by one of the youth leaders. The evening was superb—excellent cuisine, spectacular entertainment, meaningful program, and a resounding farewell. And then we went from the sublime to the ridiculous, as we headed to the nearest subway station to get our transportation home. (I couldn't afford a limo for the return trip.)

After traveling on two different subways, we eventually came to a stop in the vicinity of Kirsten's home sometime after midnight, but still had several blocks to walk. Finally we arrived, walked up several exterior steps to the partially enclosed deck, not far from the front door. We were exhausted from the long trek back from the hotel, and simply sat down on the top step. Kirsten took off her heels, spread her gown with its crinolines on the steps, and relaxed. We talked about the great evening we had experienced. Then, we closed our eyes, kissed, and sat rather motionless in the cool evening air.

Then it happened, around 2:00 a.m., when—all of a sudden—a man's deep voice coming from the bottom of the steps startled us: "Excuse me, but would you please move over; I need to put these milk bottles in that box," as he pointed to the space next to the wall.

Of course, we moved so he could complete his task. And then we looked at each other, smiled and quietly giggled. "What a story we have to tell some of our friends," I said to Kirsten.

"Think of the story he's going to tell his co-workers," she answered. We both giggled some more, smiled, and kissed good night. She thanked me for a great evening. I reiterated the same. Then she went in, and I went down the street to catch the first of two bus rides for the 40-minute trip home

EXPANDING MY SPIRITUAL JOURNEY (4)

The church became the sociological center of my life by the time I entered high school. Most of my close friends were members, or regular participants, at 59th Street Church. But a smaller, though significant number, attended Bethelship, 66th Street, and 52nd Street. In addition, some were in congregations or youth group movements outside the colony. Periodic gatherings at 59th Street included youth from a number of these sources and often numbered between 150 and 200. Weekly meetings of youth at 59th Street Church exceeded 100.

When I transferred my membership from Bethelship to 59th Street at the beginning of my sophomore year and became active in youth group meetings and activities, I solidified my sense of belonging. I did not attend after-school activities at my high school except for Trinity Club—no baseball games, theatrical performances, or musical concerts. One reason was the location of the school—a half hour bus ride away—while the church was within walking distance. Other reasons were the attachments I felt toward my close friends and the engaging activities such as our basketball teams, youth choir, and outings in which many of us participated.

Someone in our peer group distributed a poem that had a dramatic influence in my life as well as several others. The title was: "If Jesus Came to Your House." It begins with a provocative inquiry: *If Jesus came unexpectedly to your house, I wonder what you'd do.* I kept reflecting on that thought, not only for days, but for weeks—even months. I knew it was not a literal question, but it was nevertheless real for me, as I juxtaposed the historical Jesus with the risen Christ (though I wouldn't have explained it in those terms at the time).

Conversations among my friends from church were common on a variety of subjects, both serious and hilarious, though the ones pertaining to living as a follower of Jesus were most meaningful to me. The acronym WWJD? (What Would Jesus Do?) was often mentioned; but the rephrasing of it into the wording "What is Jesus asking me to do?" made it more personal. And shifting the question to "What is God asking me to do?" made it more relevant.

During my high school years I was repeatedly drawn back to an earlier Sunday evening at Bethelship Church when I was in junior high. Toward the end of that service, the pastor asked if God was speaking to anyone about "full-time Christian service." I knew what that meant; I had heard it many times. But this particular night, I sensed that God might be speaking to me. And when the pastor asked if anyone was "willing" to go into such service, I thought that might be me. I wasn't ready to make such a decision, but I was willing to consider it.

In response to the pastor's invitation, I found myself standing up. So did a couple of other youth, though not in the row where I was sitting. The atmosphere was quiet and contemplative—no music, and no emotional appeal. Just the gracious voice of a pastor inviting us to stand if we were "willing" to go into "full-time Christian service." I did a lot of thinking after that service, and talked with a number of people at that church.

Now at 59th Street Church I was continuing to reflect on that event as I contemplated what I was going to do with my life. Would my "being willing" lead to a vocation of serving in "full-time Christian service?" I didn't know, but I kept pondering it.

Ever since being introduced to the book, *In His Steps,* in junior high, I continued to think about the understanding of the gospel in both individual and social contexts. No, I didn't use that terminology until my college years, but I was perplexed and disturbed when I learned that Negroes (the term we used in the 1940s for African Americans) who were veterans, were not allowed to buy homes in Levittown (a short distance east of Brooklyn), not even make an application for one. I had heard about that post-war development in 1947—when I was 9 years old—as my father, after an evening meal, showed our family a picture on front page of the *Daily News.* He didn't mention the housing discrimination—probably didn't even know about it. All he talked about was how awful the street looked, with every house looking exactly the same as the next one, in order to sell them for a price comparable to that of renting one. It was a spectacular success for the Levitt family and the tens of thousands of Caucasians, but devastating for Negroes!

I may have been out of the loop in my junior and senior high school years, but I never heard anyone in the Norwegian colony talk about the injustices experienced by Negro people—neither the pastors nor the lay people. Perhaps their lack of awareness, coupled with their limited understanding of structures of society in a country new to them, kept them from speaking out about such a blatantly racist endeavor. For me, and at least some of my contemporaries, we have since then come to grasp the meaning of biblical justice, and to understand the gospel in social as well as personal categories.

I'm not able to speak about the overall understanding of the gospel in the Norwegian colony of the 1940s and '50s since I was not cognizant of it during the time of my growing up years, nor how that interpretation may have changed in the colony over the past 60 years. However, through my relationships over time, my observations have led me to conclude that some people in the colony continue to regard the gospel as strictly personal, while others have broadened their perspective to include both the personal and the social.

INTERACTING WITH MULTIPLE NEIGHBORHOODS (5)

Walking, riding my bike, utilizing buses, ferries, and the vast subway system, enabled me to experience all five boroughs of NYC in its diversity, not just Brooklyn. These ventures allowed me to encounter countless variations of neighborhoods, including numerous cultures, races, and languages.

My immediate neighborhood was almost like an island in a diverse city. Yet it was neither isolated from surrounding areas, nor from the many people who were not Norwegian residing within it. The colony had no firm boundaries, only a perspective that those living in the colony had. When traveling through any of these neighborhoods, I regularly assumed they would all be relatively safe. However, I learned certain guidelines throughout my upbringing to enhance my safety: "Go with someone. Be extra cautious when you're in an unfamiliar location. When it's dark, choose the lighted pathway. Take enough money to get back home, but not a lot of extra." And many more such as these.

But sometimes unexpected situations occurred, like it did one evening when I was walking home along Ninth Avenue. I had just crossed 57th Street about 9:30 p.m. Yes, I was alone, in a very familiar neighborhood, on the side of the street that was, unfortunately, rather dark (due to the tall hedges next to the narrow sidewalk), with several dollars in my wallet in my back pocket, and a bright, brass watch on my left wrist.

All at once, I was startled by two young men—one who jumped me from behind, placing his left arm around my neck, and the barrel of a gun firmly against my back, and saying in a rushed, loud voice, "Give me your wallet and your watch." At the same time, the man on my right side, was trying to grab my arm, but didn't get hold of it. And, at that very moment—as adrenalin was rushing through me—I unexpectedly hit the man on my right, as hard as I could with my right elbow in his gut, without thinking about what I was doing. I surprised both men—and myself—by what I had just done.

Suddenly, I found myself running down the sidewalk—in a zigzag manner—as fast as I could. And then, another stunning surprise, as I heard the sound of a shot, and the crackling sound of the bullet striking the three-foot-tall can, filled with ashes, at the edge of the sidewalk right next to me. I jumped between two cars on my left, running at breakneck speed, as close as I could to cars parked ahead of me, eventually cutting behind the last two cars to the sidewalk, and then around the corner. As I turned, I took a quick look down the sidewalk, but couldn't see anyone, and ran as rapidly as I could toward 932 56th Street. When I arrived, I was panting so intensely, I just stood inside the main door for several minutes, trying to catch my breath. I finally went in, greeted my mother, who asked why I was breathing so heavily—I guess I hadn't waited long enough. "I guess I was running too hard. I'm fine," I responded. I never told her what had happened. I was just grateful I got away, and still had my wallet, my watch, and my life!

Most of the experiences in my immediate neighborhood were different than that evening. They often involved sitting on a stoop at a friend's house in reasonably warm weather. One such evening toward the end of my senior year, I sat talking with Betty—one of my most trusted friends—on the front steps of her house. After some general sharing pertaining to what the future might hold for each of us, she asked me what qualities I thought would be most important in a life's partner. We had a conversation so profound that I still remember some of the important items we discussed.

But that evening did not end our conversation, because three years later, when we were both students at a midwestern university, Betty asked me if I remembered the conversation we had three years earlier. "Now that I've met your fiancée, I'm wondering how she measures up to your list of desirable qualities."

"I'm excited to tell you that she fulfills 98% of my list," I said. "I was hoping for 50%, maybe 70 or 75%. But she matches what I was hoping for far beyond my expectations. I am such a lucky guy, to find such a wonderful life's partner."

Many of the experiences my Norwegian friends and I had were very similar to what my Italian friends and their families had. We shared with each other, and realized our similarities regarding human relationships were not unique to one ethnic group. The same was true for my Jewish friends, as well as other cultural groups. Such an awareness helped each of us realize we were not superior, or inferior, to others with whom we associated. It also enabled us to reach across cultural boundaries. This meant that when I went to the roller-skating, or ice-skating rink, I would choose a gal to skate the "couples only" number with me because she was an excellent skater, or was attractive, or both. I wouldn't necessarily choose a gal because she was Norwegian. And that sometimes irritated some of the Norwegian gals, which I secretly enjoyed.

A connection I never made, except in superficial ways, was with the Sons of Norway groups at various locations in Brooklyn. The primary reason, from my perspective, was that the social life of most, though not all, of the parents from the four churches to which I related was so heavily focused on church-related activities that they didn't have time to become involved in other programs. Furthermore, children and youth from these churches were not given opportunities to relate to their peers in that group. Though I am saddened that I wasn't able to include relationships with those from the Sons of Norway, I have since that time become an active member of the organization.

Interacting with other neighborhoods took place in ways too vast to include in this narrative. However, some of the most prominent celebrities who grew up in the vicinity of my home and high school include Janet Yellen (Secretary of the Treasury), Bernard King (NBA Hall of Fame inductee), and Paul Jabara (singer and songwriter), all of whom graduated from Fort Hamilton High School as I did. Others were Martin Adler (developer of the Brooklyn Dodgers Hall of Fame) who was my classmate; Pee Wee Reese and Duke Snider (Dodgers—Worlds Series champions), who lived within walking distance to my high school; Anthony Fauci (infectious disease specialist) who worked with his father in a drugstore on a street where I used to ride my bike, and Barbra Streisand (singer) who attended Erasmus High

School where I rode my bike as well. Hundreds of other celebrities, too numerous to mention, also came from Brooklyn.

DISCOVERING OTHER SIMILAR COLONIES (6)

Small groups of residents from the Norwegian colony in Brooklyn established what some of them called "Little Norway" in areas surrounding Brooklyn. They were often locations in the countryside of New Jersey and Long Island—like my parents and some friends had properties in Connecticut. Three of these communities, among more than a dozen, were in New Jersey at Lake Telemark, Sunset Hill, and Norsville.

The one at Lake Telemark was the largest (as far as I can ascertain). It included a beautiful lake with numerous cabins along the shore as well as in the surrounding hillsides. The parents of one of my close neighborhood friends, Marty, had a bungalow up the hill from the lake. One year during Christmas break from school, Marty, Roy (another friend from Brooklyn), and I spent a few days there when the temperatures were well below freezing. After we arrived, we started a fire in the cast iron, potbelly stove, loading it with as much wood as it would hold. Hours later, the living room, where we had unrolled our sleeping bags, was toasty warm. After the sun had set, we bundled up and went ice-skating on the frozen lake—racing against each other, forward and backward—until it was late, and we were the only ones remaining on the ice. The serene atmosphere, the hushed stillness, and the moon shining through the bare branches of the trees made for a spectacular time. Knowing that a warm bungalow, milk and chocolate that would soon become hot chocolate, gave us a tranquil vision that would soon become a reality.

Two other Norwegian communities also had cottages that were connected to our peer group. One was in Sunset Hill, where Lita's parents had a bungalow that hosted more than a dozen of us for a marvelous summer weekend. Another was in Norsville, where Barbara's grandparents had a bungalow that hosted a group of us for another superb weekend! We had so much fun during each of these weekends.

Although my parents' cabin in Connecticut didn't have enough beds for such a large group, there were summer weekends with some of those same friends. One was the time Rolf and I wanted to bring our electric guitars and amplifiers, play and sing together outside, at a volume loud enough to reach other cabins across the valley. Rolf invited Ruth, and I invited Kirsten, and to have a vehicle to get there, we asked Bob (one of our youth leaders), his wife and baby to go with us. My parents were gracious to load all our musical gear into their car. And what a great weekend we had—at the lake, at the cabin, and on the walks we took up and down the hillsides. And, of course, all the delicious food my mother prepared and served.

On a subsequent occasion, following a gala in a Manhattan hotel that celebrated the end of our senior year, Don (another of our youth leaders), his friend, and Barbara, my friend, traveled to my parents' home in Connecticut for a weekend. In addition to the fun we had at the lake and the cabin, we had some deep and meaningful conversations pertaining to our respective futures. Don was considering becoming a missionary in a country overseas, and his friend was trying to discern her future. Barbara was not planning to go away to college, and would be pursuing studies locally. I was in the process of working through plans to attend a midwestern university that had accepted me. However, each of us was desirous of discerning where God was leading us, not only in the next step, but in the choice of a vocation that we thought would be a life-time decision. Little did we know that life often provides opportunities to serve in more than one career.

In addition to small groups of Norwegians gathering in groups in the vicinity surrounding NYC, larger groups went to summer resorts for a week, or several weeks, within reasonable driving distances farther away. One of those locations was Camp-of-the-Woods, a couple of hundred miles upstate, in Speculator, New York. I worked there on the staff throughout the summer of 1954, when I was sixteen years old. Since it was known more for its inspirational speakers and music concerts than the beautiful white sandy beach, those who sought staff positions had to qualify by completing forms, gathering references, and auditioning for acceptance into the chorale and/or the concert band.

One of the major events of the week was the Saturday evening concert that featured soloists, ensembles, the chorale, and the band. The performances were not fully in the professional category, but came close to this level in a number of selections performed. Surprise elements would sometimes occur.

At one Saturday night show, the first chair trumpeter had an apparent disagreement with the director, stood up, argued with him, and walked out the side door. The director was so flustered, he whispered to some band members, since the next number on the program was "The Bugler's Holiday," in which the trumpeter, who had just walked out, had the solo part, as stated in the program. However, the director raised the baton, and the band started playing. When it came time for the solo, a beam of bright light struck the rear door at the top of a long set of stairs, as the trumpeter stepped out and sounded the first note—to the thunderous applause of the audience. (Many of us on stage were just as fooled as those in the audience.)

That summer was a great experience for me, not only with those on the staff, but with the hundreds of wonderful guests from churches and related institutions throughout New York and surrounding states—who, by the way, tipped their servers very well! Yes, I served tables, family style, at all meals, but also sang in the chorale, and participated in numerous other activities. Amidst all the fun I had, I most enjoyed water skiing—singles, doubles, and triples—a sport that I hadn't learned until that summer. And the time I enjoyed the most, was when Tom and I decided to ski doubles on a windy, cold afternoon, starting from a sitting position on the pier, wearing dry sweatshirts, to see if we could both start without getting wet. We made it, gave each other a "thumbs up," and criss-crossed several times on our way toward the other end of the lake. When we were starting to head back, I thought it was my turn to play a trick on Tom. I owed him one! So I got his attention, waved, and let go of the rope, while making it look like I lost my grip. Of course, the boat slowed, turned around to pick us up, both of us soaking wet in our sweatshirts. When the driver asked what happened, I was laughing so much, I couldn't respond. Tom answered, "I think I know what happened." And then he looked at me and said, "Just wait; I'll get you next time."

LEARNING IN HIGH SCHOOL – FORT HAMILTON 490 (7)

In the fall of 1952, when I was 14 years old, I enrolled at Fort Hamilton High School, located at 8301 Shore Road, overlooking the section of the Hudson River called The Narrows. The view from the school, especially from the exterior side facing the harbor, was a daily treat.

I took a city bus from the corner of 57th Street and Fort Hamilton Parkway each morning. It came to that location, and then remained there for ten minutes, while a number of students from the neighborhood arrived and boarded. Several were my friends, though anyone could board. The ride along thirty city streets, and several long blocks, took about half an hour—long enough to engage in all sorts of interesting conversations.

Students were in either 10th, 11th, or 12th grade. There were no longer *special* classes like the ones I had experienced in junior high. Approximately 90% of the students were Caucasian when I attended, but that percentage has decreased to 36%, with 32% Hispanic, 28% Asian, and 4% African American. The current enrollment is 4,600 (for four years), while it was approximately 1,900 (for three years) when I attended.

In class I usually sat near the front, paid attention, listened carefully, and took detailed notes on what seemed important. I didn't study much at home except for writing papers and reports, organizing information in notebooks, and studying for exams—often with friends who were earning high grades. At lunch I chose to sit with more than a dozen girls at "Table E." We often brought our own lunch, though some of us—yes, I was one of them—also mooched off other students' lunches. We had so much fun during that period!

In my sophomore class of more than 600 students, we had close to 10% who were members of an honor society called *Arista.* I had the privilege of being one of them. However, the number of Norwegians was relatively small. I've sometimes wondered if those of us who had parents with a limited educational background did not receive the extent of academic assistance at home that other students did. What they did provide was an abundance of authentic love, caring support, and wise counsel, qualities that turned out to be incredibly important.

I was also a member of the Mixed Chorus, the number one singing group in our high school. My dear friend, Barbara, was accompanist. Our director was Mrs. Salzberg, who believed in our musical ability so deeply that she worked it out for our chorus to cut a record—yes, the large 78 rpm version—that featured a variety of selections. I was excited when she invited me to be a soloist in one of them. With her interest in what might develop as a musical career, she encouraged me to study voice with a professional coach. I did accept her advice and took voice lessons for a few months during my senior year in high school. (I still enjoy singing "O Sole Mio" in the shower, particularly when the walls are made from resonating materials such as marble).

When our class reached the last year, we had our senior pictures taken (photo on back cover). We also had a Senior Assembly. Over 600 classmates elected two as Class Singers, one male and one female. I was one, and Carol Knudsen, an attractive Norwegian girl with a superb singing voice, was the other. After we each performed a solo in the early part of the program, we sang a duet just before the program ended: "Deep in my heart, dear, I have a dream of you," from Student Prince (a current movie at that time), featuring Mario Lanza singing that number in the movie. Yes, for those few moments I became Mario Lanza (at least to myself).

When we were introduced and came out from behind the curtain, our fellow classmates, together with our teachers, administrators, and guests, greeted us with enthusiastic applause. As the pianist played the introduction, I turned to Carol and smiled as genuinely as I could; she smiled delicately in return. And then I began to sing these lines of the refrain as I looked into her eyes:

Deep in my heart, dear, I have a dream of you.
Fashioned in starlight, fragrant with roses and dew.

Carol, in her magnificently trained voice, responded:

Our paths may sever, but I'll remember forever;
Deep in my heart, dear, I'll always dream of you.

Then, after singing two verses as alternating solos, we joined our voices together at the end, singing the refrain once again as a duet in unison:

Deep in my heart, dear, I have a dream of you.
Fashioned in starlight, fragrant with roses and dew.

And then, blending our voices in harmonious tones, we turned toward each other, and sang:

Our paths may sever, but I'll remember forever;
Deep in my heart, dear, I'll always dream of you.

As we concluded, we received a thunderous expression of joy and celebration from the audience. From my perspective, it was not only for our duet, but for Carol's fabulous voice—so well trained and expertly performed. It was a privilege for me to sing with her on that occasion.

The only humorous part of this event (at least for me) was that Carol was three inches taller than me. However, as we rehearsed, our singing coach, who was one of the music teachers, made suggestions of stances and movements that minimized this height differential.

Our class celebrated graduation on June 29, 1955. It was a different time in many ways. One was in the music that was chosen for that event. It included "God of Our Fathers" as the opening hymn, and two musical selections sung by the Mixed Chorus, "The Hallelujah Chorus" from "The Messiah," and the spiritual, "Climbin' Up the Mountain."

I received two awards that day. One was the Phi Beta Kappa Alumni Award. Although the award was announced from the podium with the other awards, a woman representing the New York chapter sought me out after the ceremony was over to congratulate me, and to emphasize how prestigious this award was. Several teachers, administrators, and classmates also came to congratulate me. My parents did not have much understanding of it, but they were duly impressed. I learned that day it was for the boy with the highest GPA. The girl with the highest GPA was recognized with an award called the "Scholastic Award," a clear expression of a sexist action, especially when I later learned that she, and three other girls, had fractionally higher GPAs than I did. However, no one (including me) seemed cognizant of that injustice at the time.

I also received the Social Studies Award, given to one boy and one girl (the same two of us who had received the scholarship awards).

ENGAGING IN ACTIVITIES BEYOND SCHOOL (8)

Of my many activities during my junior and senior high school years, one that stood out was my connection to the Brooklyn Dodgers, including my ventures to Ebbetts Field where they played their home games. I became familiar with many of the players by name, as I listened avidly to games on the radio, and looked at individual, large photos of the players on my bedroom walls. But most exciting was seeing them on their field during batting practice in the mornings (although the games were in the afternoon).

Those among my friends who also were avid fans, would go with me down the aisles along the third base line to rows of empty seats near the front, to get as close as we could to the players. *Did the stadium workers tell us we weren't allowed to be there?* Of course—constantly! *Did we leave?* Only temporarily, so we wouldn't get caught and thrown out. *Did we get chased again?* Yes, but we never got caught. We had learned to jump across one or more rows of seats. Sometimes, the older men left us alone, after they saw we weren't causing any damage, and the ticket holders had not yet arrived. *Did we love yelling out players' names, and having them wave to us—even tossing a ball our way occasionally?* Certainly! And we did this, game after game, during the season.

According to tradition, the Dodgers got their name from the trolley cars that pedestrians often had to dodge when crossing a major thoroughfare. They were initially called the Trolley Dodgers, though the word *trolley* soon disappeared. As their popularity increased, people in Brooklyn not only cheered for them, they also lived by them.

In the late 1940s and early '50s, a number of players lived in or near the Bay Ridge section of Brooklyn. Pee Wee Reese lived at 9714 Barwell Terrace, off 97th Street, between Third and Fourth Avenues. Duke Snider's residence was in the same neighborhood at 143 Marine Avenue. Both of these homes were within walking distance to my high school. Gil Hodges' home, only a short distance away, was on Bradford Avenue, between Avenue M and Avenue N. These three players—shortstop, center fielder, first baseman—and several others, had numerous honors, not only on the team, but in the entire league.

Then, one summer day, a distinctive surprise happened while my friends and I were playing stickball on Tenth Avenue, between 58th and 59th Streets, a short street without houses on either side. A black Cadillac sedan pulled up in what we had designated as the outfield. We paused and looked, unable to figure out why the car had stopped. After several seconds, both front doors opened and two men stepped out and started walking toward us. All of a sudden, we recognized that they were Roy Campanella and Pee Wee Reese, the Dodgers' catcher and shortstop! We were thrilled to see them. We ran to greet them, and talked with them for several minutes. Then Campy said, "All right, let's see you play."

At that moment, I realized it was my turn to bat. I picked up my mother's mop handle, and a Spauldeen, and got up to hit. I connected, hitting a hot grounder to third, and beating the throw to first base. We continued to play until we reached a third out. Then, Pee Wee stepped forward and asked, "Who hit the shot to third base." I responded that it was me. He picked up the stick, held his hands in a somewhat different angle than I did, and then looking directly at me, said, "Try it like this," demonstrating what he had just told us, "And you'll get more power behind your shot." Our discussion continued until the two of them had to leave. We thanked them, shook their hands, and waved goodbye. Then we sat down and processed—at length—what had just occurred.

When I got home, I shared what had happened, and then said to my mother, "I want to keep this handle that Pee Wee Reese held in his own hands. I'll buy you a new one." She nodded, and smiled. I gave her a hug, and whispered, "Thanks."

The Dodgers were my heroes! They won their first World Series in 1955, the year I graduated from high school (though I was in Indiana, beginning my first year in college). My mother sent me the front page of the Daily News. It had a sketch of the face of an unshaven, unkempt vagrant with a wide-open mouth featuring his one tooth. The headline read: "Who's a Bum?"

Scores of other exciting events took place during my high school years, but space will permit me to include only three of them. The first was a two-day bike trip that my friend, Ivar, and I took to *Tante Dagny* and *Oncle Olaf's* home in Rye, New York, on balloon tire bikes, and no gearshift to assist us. We started at 932 56th Street—my apartment—on a beautiful, summer morning. We left about 7:00 a.m., and headed directly for the Staten Island ferry at 69th Street. After a refreshing trip across The Narrows, we transferred to the Manhattan Ferry and enjoyed the ride past the Statue of Liberty to the City (the name people in other boroughs called Manhattan). Then the arduous task of traveling up Broadway, through the financial district, Times Square, and Central Park began. There was so much to see, and so much to digest, that it was difficult not to stop and simply absorb details of the environment. But we had to keep going, except for drinks of water along the way. We finally left Manhattan, crossed over the Harlem River, and entered the Bronx—home of the Yankees. After we had eaten lunch under a shady tree, we continued through communities in Westchester County. In late afternoon we finally arrived at our destination, tired and sore from all the sitting, but excited that we had safely arrived. We celebrated over a sumptuous meal, showered, and went early to bed, aware that we had to ride the same exhausting route back to Brooklyn the next day!

The second was an event that occurred the evening of December 31 during each of my high school years. It took place in Manhattan, in the vicinity of 42nd Street and Broadway. Many of my friends and I began our venture between 8 and 9 p.m. outside of Dodenhoff's. We then continued by subway to Times Square. The atmosphere was quite festive, even before we reached our destination. Once we climbed the stairs to reach street level, we saw people everywhere, some dressed in high society fashion, others in the weirdest attire you could imagine, while most looked rather typical.

As the hour moved toward midnight, the crowd increased in size, the peddlers of watches and other flashing jewelry became more aggressive, and the need to empty bladders intensified almost uncontrollably. Everyone's attention turned to the bright light atop the pole at One Times Square. Then, with 60 seconds remaining before midnight, the ball slowly dropped until it hit bottom, and the blazing lights of the numbers of the new year appeared—jointly with loud noises of all sorts, human voices expressing all types of sentiment, bodies holding and hugging whomever was nearby, and confetti flying down from the tops of tall buildings! And then all kinds of activities took place for hours—there, on our way back, and after we arrived in Bay Ridge—some years until the light of dawn appeared!!!

The third was a series of excursions we took to parks in the boroughs of NYC. The favorite for everyone in my peer group was Coney Island—442 acres along the sandy beach and ocean waves; with foods such as Nathan's world-famous frankfurters, with thick ripple cuts of deep-fried potatoes, and Hirsch's Knishes; games of all sorts to play along the 80-foot-wide boardwalk; spectacular fireworks at least one night a week; and rides galore! And it was the rides that we loved the most: four roller coasters, especially the Cyclone with all of its speed, sharp turns, and steep descents; the gigantic Wonder Wheel; the incredible 250-foot-tall-Parachute Jump; and so much more. It was always a lot of fun to see which guy was going to take which gal on one or more of the rides! Although last, but certainly not least, was all the fun we had on the beach, and in the wonderful salt water! I loved that place and went as often as I could. It took only one subway ride to get there—the Sea Beach Express—with ongoing departures, 24/7, from 62nd Street and Eighth Avenue.

Other parks included Central Park—840 acres in the center of Manhattan, 59th to 110th Streets, between Fifth Avenue and Central Park West. It was regarded as a masterpiece of landscape architecture, with magnificent buildings surrounding a lake. Rowing a rental boat on that lake, while viewing the breath-taking landscape and the surrounding structural architecture, was most impressive for me and others in our peer group.

Alley Pond Park in Queens (655 acres), and Van Cortlandt Park in the Bronx (more than 1,000 acres), were destinations for our entire youth group from 59th Street Church. Since they were full-day outings—filled with sports and other activities—we brought our lunches and other goodies with us. It was a reasonable length subway ride to Alley Pond, but quite a long trip to Van Cortlandt—traveling through a part of Brooklyn, all of Manhattan, and part of Bronx. However, wherever our group was—even on a long subway ride, we always had a good time.

A memorable trip for me, and many from our youth group, was the annual early summer trip to Bear Mountain State Park. We first traveled to midtown Manhattan by subway, then boarded a large sightseeing boat, and sailed up the Hudson River to Bear Mountain on the west bank of the river—about 50 miles north of NYC. While there, we hiked on trails, walked through woods, and eventually got to the tower at the top of the mountain. Views of the river below, as well as other locations in the mountains, made for great experiences, especially when discussed with close friends.

When we heard the loud horns sounding several times from our boat coming back down the river, we knew we had better be close to the end of the trails at the river's edge, or we'd have to find other transportation home.

GROWING UP: BROADENING MY VALUES (9)

As I have already shared, a sense of values rather than rules governed my behavior. I don't know the extent to which my parents realized this, but I do know I wasn't consciously aware of this approach as I was growing up, particularly in my early years.

The most central values had their points of convergence in God's will for our lives. That awareness was portrayed in a life-size painting of Jesus kneeling beside a large stone, and looking upward, as he had done in the Garden of Gethsemane. It covered the central portion of the front wall of the lower auditorium in 59th Street Church. Every time I walked in, or soon thereafter, my eyes were drawn to that location. Furthermore, at other times in the service, especially during the time someone was at the podium (located at the left side of the painting), I would glance—sometimes stare—at it. It was a constant reminder of words Jesus had prayed: "Not my will, but your will be done."

This focus was also at the core of my parents' values. They didn't say these words very often, but they attempted to live by them—day after day. In doing so, they left the application of them up to me, even in practical details of everyday life: "Don't stay out too late," rather than "Be home by 10." Or, "Go with someone," rather than, "Who are you going with?" Or, "Have a good time," rather than, "Where are you going?" And, rather frequently, "Follow whatever you think Jesus wants you to do," rather than, "Don't do this," or, "Don't do that."

This way of helping me make my own decisions grew out of my parents' wisdom, even though they had a limited formal education. It gave me a great deal of freedom, while at the same time, provided me with values that became my guidelines for making decisions.

This way of living was also reinforced by several close friends in my peer group, since they were attempting to live by the same, or similar, values. When I went out with a date, her parents usually—though not always—would say, "Don't get home too late." They trusted their daughter, and me, to make reasonable decisions. More than once a parent said to me as we were about to go out the front door, "When you take out our daughter, we know you'll take good care of her." Although neither they, nor I, understood the sexist attitude of such a statement, they meant they trusted me to act wisely in their behalf. I can even remember one parent saying, "When you take our daughter out, I can go to bed and not worry."

The meaningful relationships I had with those in my

peer group meant that I also had the same basic connections with their parents. It was common to visit my friends in their homes. On occasion, those same friends came to my home, in Connecticut as well as Brooklyn. It was like having one large family—all living by similar values. In addition to where we lived, we met many others from the colony at church meetings, school functions, stores, parks, and a variety of community events such as parades and rallies.

Permeating these varied occasions were numerous common values that were centered in a deep sense of caring for one another's well-being. Mutual kindness was not only expressed, but was expected. Honesty and truth-telling was not only assumed, but found consistently in one another's transactions. A high regard for nature was prevalent in all circumstances, but especially in parks and the countryside outside of Brooklyn.

The broadening of such values varied with individuals and groups outside the Norwegian colony, depending to a large extent on the experiences of each person and family. However, the acceptance of others with differences in language, ethnic origins, and/or cultural practices did not necessarily dissuade members of the colony from expressing their values toward them, though sometimes with an initial sense of caution. Those of us who were in the Norwegian colony often realized that the ones outside the colony were far more similar to us, than they were different!

DEVELOPING TRUST IN GOD (AND GOD'S TRUST IN ME) (10)

I first experienced trust in my mother and father, and their trust in me, in my pre-school years. In my grade school years, I learned to trust others in the colony, and received their trust in me. I developed a deep trust in myself during my junior high years. And in my senior high school years, I entered into a profound relationship with God that involved not only my trust in God, but God's trust in me.

The verse from the Bible that spoke to me most powerfully was Proverbs 3:5-6: "Trust in the Lord with all your heart, and do not rely on your own insight. In all your ways acknowledge him, and he will make straight your paths." I memorized it, and referred to it numerous times—when I was by myself, and when I was with others. However, my understanding was related to my trust in God. What I came to realize, rather slowly, was that a relationship of trust cannot be one-sided, because a relationship—by definition—is between two entities. Therefore, could it be that if I trusted God, and we had a trust relationship, that God also trusted me?

That way of thinking *blew my mind*. At first, I felt I couldn't even dare to believe such a possibility! It was such an overwhelming thought: That God would trust a human being? That God would trust me? I reflected on this, long and hard—for hours, for days. Finally, I said to myself: *Perhaps*. And then I followed that thought with the words: *No way*. It even sounded presumptuous to raise that possibility. But over many days—and weeks—I meditated, and with a profound sense of humility, I prayed, earnestly and fervently, seeking God's wisdom on the matter. I finally said to myself: *Perhaps. Maybe not. But perhaps.*

I kept this possibility to myself for months, *thinking about what God might have in mind by trusting a human being—by trusting me*. I slowly drew a tentative question: If God has chosen to work through people—which I believed he has—then perhaps God is willing to trust people to carry out what he leads them to do. Perhaps God is willing to trust me to do what he is calling me to do. *WOW, I thought. That's almost unbelievable! But that's also incredibly humbling!*

As a senior in high school, I would not have been able to articulate this understanding as fully as I have stated it here. Nevertheless, it was an emerging thought at this point in my maturity, one that continued to come to fuller fruition during my years in college and graduate school.

The application of this understanding of God's trust in me, coupled with my willingness to go into "full-time Christian service," led me to specific questions: Who does God want me to be? What does God want me to do? What are the next steps I should take, after graduating from high school? And the most pertinent question: How does God want me to live right now?

I diligently thought about questions such as these when I was alone. Or, at other times when I was in conversation with a friend, or a group of friends. Or, still other times, when I was in a church service, or participating in a church-related activity. Possibilities of all sorts surfaced, ranging from the likely to the unlikely. Yet, the comforting response when I didn't know, or couldn't even come close to knowing, was my trust relationship with God.

I learned to pray more wisely, and more fully. Often, I would spend time thanking God for being a God of steadfast love, regardless of what might happen to me, and the world of which I was a part. In addition, I would ask God for wisdom and direction, regarding present living, and future possibilities. And in the midst of such prayers, I would praise God for the privilege of trusting him, and seek God's guidance in understanding what he was trusting me to do, and the manner in which he was trusting me to do it. I was learning to trust in the Lord with all my heart, and to use my own insight, but not solely rely on it!

APPENDICES

HISTORICAL DEVELOPMENT OF THE COLONY

MAPS AND LOCATIONS

NORWEGIAN STORES ON EIGHTH AVENUE

SECTIONS OF CHAPTERS

READER'S REFLECTION

HISTORICAL DEVELOPMENT OF THE COLONY

The beginning of Norwegian immigration to the United States took place the 4th of July 1825, when the "sloop" RESTAURATION left Stavanger, Norway, for the US. However, many of those passengers continued to Kendall, in Orleans County, in upstate New York. Forty years later, in 1865, the first mass migration of more than 100,000 Norwegians occurred, and most of them also continued to the Midwest.

The second mass migration occurred in 1880 when Norway suffered a great depression. At the same time, there was a transition from sail to steam. Many of the young sailors who came "jumped ship" and stayed in New York.

The first colony of Norwegians in the Northeast was in Manhattan, in an area bounded by the Brooklyn Bridge, Manhattan Bridge, and the East River. In the late 1800s, the population of New York increased, technology advanced, the East River was spanned by bridge and ferry. Industries seeking more space began to move out of Manhattan. Brooklyn replaced Manhattan as the shipbuilding, ship repairing, and docking center. This increasing waterfront business provided even more work for Norwegians. By the 1870s, the Norwegian population began to migrate to the first Brooklyn settlement—*Old South Brooklyn*—near the shipping activity in Red

Hook, where men could walk to work, or commute easily to Manhattan.

The third mass migration of Norwegians—more than 200,000—occurred in 1900. Many of them settled in this first Norwegian community in Brooklyn. The churches followed the people to Brooklyn. The church was very important to the Norwegian immigrant and provided social and charitable benefits as well as religious activities.

One of these churches was the Bethel Ship which was originally a ship moored off a dock in Red Hook. This church later moved to a regular building on Carroll Street before following the next migration to Bay Ridge. The Norwegian Seamans Church was a place where young seamen could find a place to stay. It originally started in a small building and then moved to the corner of Clinton Street and First Place. In addition to a brownstone building next door, the church had a huge basement and could house over two hundred sailors, especially during World War II.

This downtown settlement lasted through the 1920s. Two factors contributed to the Norwegian immigrants moving out from *Downtown Brooklyn* as they called it: the fact that new docks and warehouses began to extend out to 59th Street, and the completion of the Fourth Avenue subway in 1915. This move was out to what was at the time called Bay Ridge, but is now called Sunset Park, mainly from Fourth Avenue to Ninth Avenue, from 44th Street to 60th Street.

Although the Norwegian Seamans Church stayed in *Downtown Brooklyn,* most of the other churches moved out to Bay Ridge, and other churches were also established there. These churches included Bethelship Norwegian Methodist Episcopal Church on Fourth Avenue and 56th Street, Trinity Lutheran Church on Fourth Avenue and 46th Street, Our Savior's Lutheran Church on Fourth Avenue and 80th Street, the

Norwegian Evangelical Lutheran Free Church on 59th Street near Eighth Avenue.

In addition to the many churches that were established, there were other important charitable institutions. Sister Elizabeth Fedde, a Norwegian immigrant, established the Norwegian Relief Society, and opened a deaconess house and nine bed hospital, that later expanded to become the Norwegian Hospital at Fourth Avenue and 44th Street. This institution became the Lutheran Medical Center of Brooklyn and still exists in the Sunset Park area. The Norwegian Children's Home was established in Bay Ridge to care for Norwegian orphans and other children whose parents could not care for them. The Norwegian Christian Home for the Aged was founded in 1903, and continues today as the Norwegian Christian Home and Health Center.

Fraternal organizations were also founded. Several Sons of Norway Lodges were established in Brooklyn, two of which carry on to this day: Lodge Brooklyn and Faerder Lodge, the oldest Lodge on the East Coast, having been established in 1911. There was also the Norwegian Engineer's Society, as well as several sporting clubs. The Gjoa Sporting Club still exists on 62nd Street near Eighth Avenue. Many Norwegians were carpenters, or worked in the construction industry, and were active in the Carpenters Union and the Dock Builder's Union.

After World War II, things were very difficult in Norway. Norwegian Americans sent care packages of clothing and food to their relatives back home. Another group of immigrants came to Brooklyn—young men who also went into carpentry and construction, and young women who became au pairs, housekeepers, seamstresses, etc. In many cases, wives and children followed their husbands here.

Eighth Avenue was the center of the Norwegian community. Grocery stores, bakeries, and restaurants dominated

Eighth Avenue (known as *Lapskaus Boulevard*—named after a Norwegian stew). Bay Ridge High School offered Norwegian as one of its foreign languages.

The peak of the Norwegian community in Bay Ridge lasted through the 1950s. After that, the children of immigrants, and immigrants themselves, moved in scattered directions—to Staten Island, New Jersey, New York (north of the city), Long Island, and Connecticut. However, there is still a Norwegian influence in Bay Ridge and Sunset Park!

MAPS AND LOCATIONS

Five Boroughs Of New York City

During the years I lived in Brooklyn (1938-55), transportation was by bicycle, subway, bus, and car (if someone else was driving) to Queens, Manhattan, and Bronx. The ferry was the only way to get to and from Staten Island.

Borough Of Brooklyn

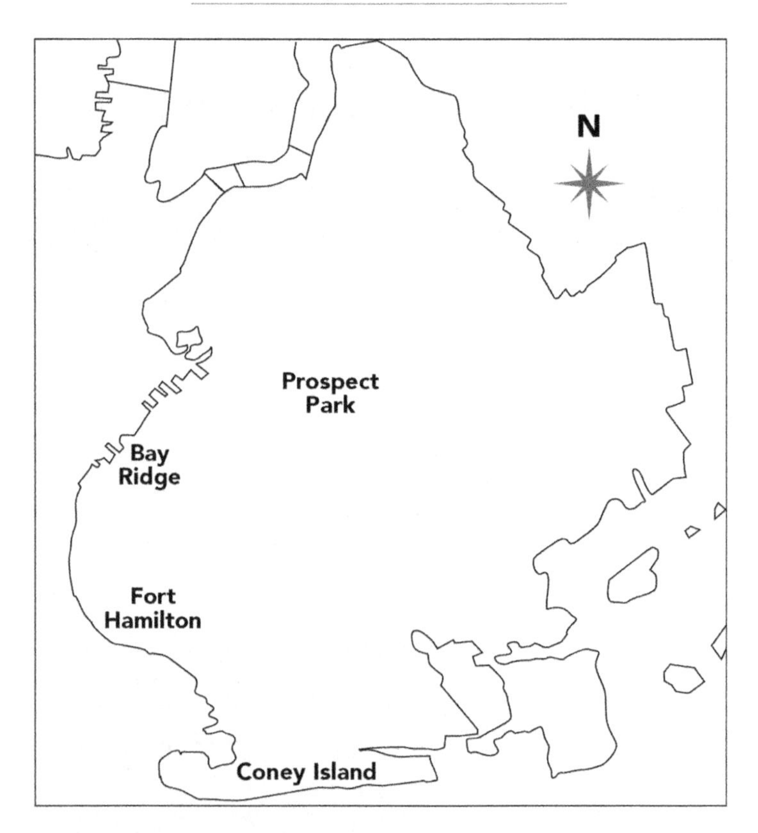

After I moved away from Brooklyn in 1955, the Verrazzano-Narrows Bridge was built (1959-64), extending Interstate 278 from New Jersey, through Staten Island, to Brooklyn, displacing 7,500 residents, and dividing the former Bay Ridge neighborhood into two separate identities, Bay Ridge and Sunset Park.

Bay Ridge And Sunset Park

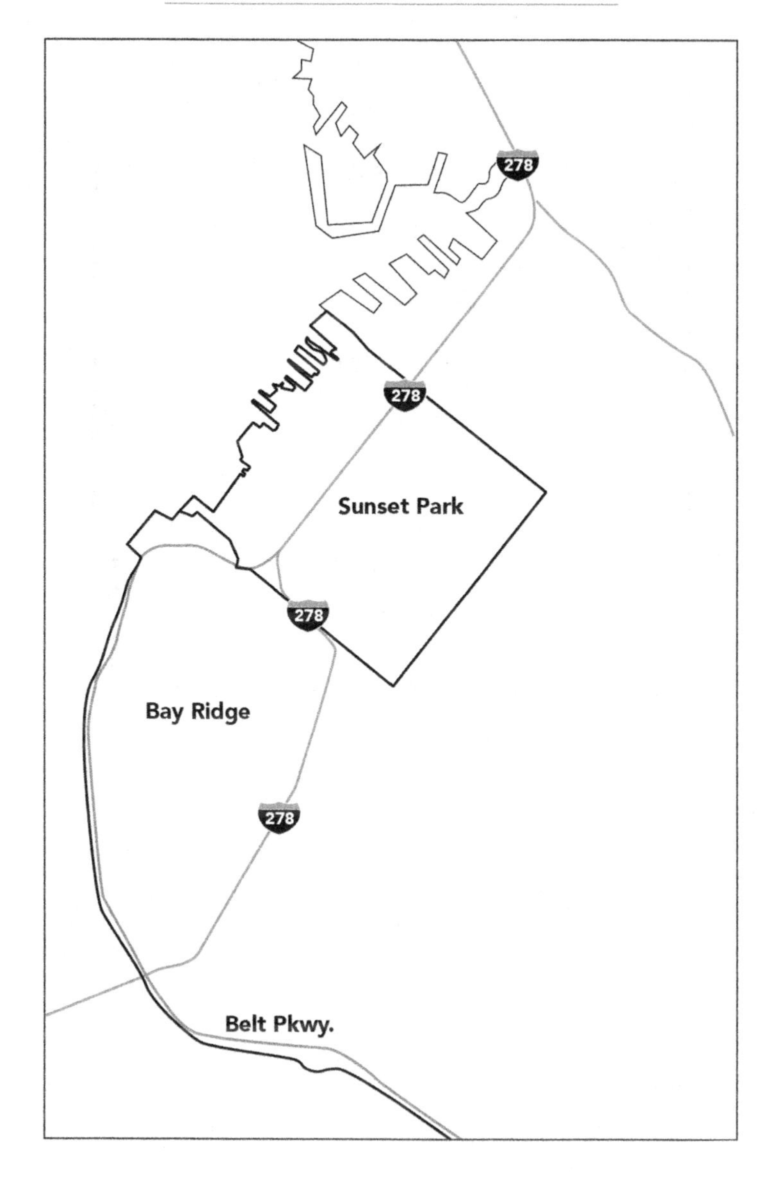

Sunset Park Neighborhood

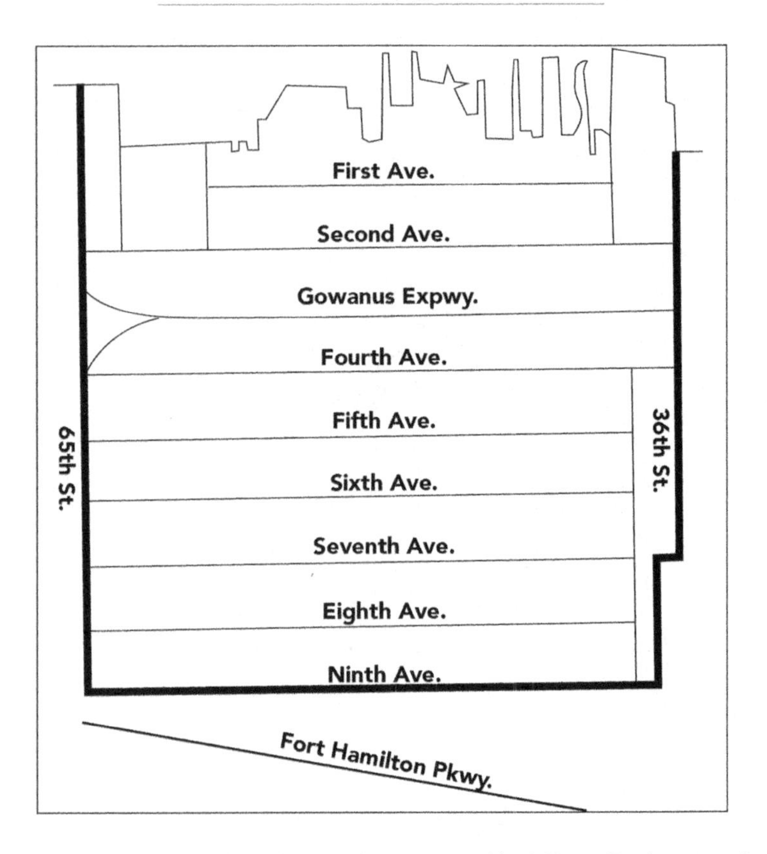

Those of us who lived in what we called Bay Ridge in the 1940s and '50s realize most people today call the northern part of that neighborhood, Sunset Park. Whatever name is used, the streets are still the same.

Locations Where I Grew Up

The following descriptions, and the preceding street maps, provide a visual framework for understanding more clearly the stories in each of the chapters. They identify apartments where I lived, schools I attended, churches of which I was a part, subway stations I used, and parks where I played.

Apartments

- 818 56th Street
- 859 44th Street
- 932 56th Street

Schools

- Public School 169 (4395 Seventh Avenue)
- Pershing Junior High School (4812 Ninth Avenue)
- Fort Hamilton High School (8301 Shore Road)

Churches

- Bethelship (corner of 56th Street and Fourth Avenue)
- 59th Street (near corner of Eighth Avenue)
- 52nd Street (corner of Eighth Avenue)
- 66th Street (corner of Sixth Avenue)

Subways

- Primary station (62nd Street and Eighth Avenue)
- Other stations (45th, 53rd, and 59th Street and Fourth Avenue)

Parks

- Sunset Park (41st to 44th Street, and Fifth to Seventh Avenue)
- Leif Erickson Park (fluctuating over time from 65th to 67th Street, and Fourth Avenue to Fort Hamilton Parkway)

- Owls Head (also known as Bliss Park, 68th Street and Shore Road/Colonial Road)
- Prospect Park (area northeast of Sunset Park)
- Shore Road Park (elongated strip of land alongside the harbor)
- Coney Island (segment of land along the southern coast of the borough), easily reached by a subway ride on the Sea Beach Express from 62nd Street and Eighth Avenue)

NORWEGIAN STORES ON EIGHTH AVENUE

54th to 60th Street

54th to 55th Street

Deer Head Cabin, Kirsten's Beauty Salon, Lorensen Fish Products, John Odegaard Radio Service, Olsen's TV, Atlantic-Sonya Restaurant, Knud Tornquist & Son Plumbing and Heating, Williamsen Real Estate and Insurance

55th to 56th Street

Arnold Bjornholm Delicatessen, Bergen's Bakery (Mellivol's), Ekeland and Berntsen Music Store, Eric's Place, Hagen and Helmers Electrical Contractors, Kallevig's Bar, Olson Diner, Scandinavian American Barber Shop

56th to 57th Street

Bob's Candy Store, Carl's Bar, Gus' Candy Store, Leif Erikson Restaurant, Norse Delicatessen, Odegaard's TV, Sorlandet"s Restaurant, Thor Krogh's Viking House, Trunz Meats

57th to 58th Street

Andersen's Candy Store, Andersen's Scandinavian Delicacies (Specialty: Lutefisk), Bay Ridge Brokerage (Reyersen), Bob's Open Kitchen, Ericksen's Florist, Fredericksen & Hagen

(Butcher), Gjoa Clubhouse, Hagen Meat Market, Harry's Bar, John Andersen Stationery and Greeting Cards, Johnsen and Ryersen, K. Johnson Bread and Cake Bakery, Norman Jewelers, Norsemen Moving and Storage, Nor-Ski Jewelers, Olson's Bakery, Oslo Restaurant, Scandia Floor Covering, Ruving's Bar and Restaurant

58th to 59th Street
Arlene's Specialty Shop, Benson Hardware, Casey and Sig (Meat and Poultry), Caspersen's Butcher Shop, Eighth Ave. Restaurant, George's Department Store, Hans Gjertsen's Electrical Contractor, Johnson's Candy Store, Levenson's Drug Store, Lund Electric, Meyer's Ice Cream Parlor, Petersen's Deli, Sandnes Dry Goods, Stemberg's 5 & 10

59th to 60th Street
Dodenhoff's Confectionery and Luncheonette, Einar Strange Radio and Supplies, Erik Olson's Bakery, Hannah Simonsen Hand-knitted Sweaters, Remmers & Christensen Curtains and Draperies, Stoutland Real Estate & Insurance, Petersen's bake Shop, Thomas Olsen & Son (Oil, Heating, and Air Conditioning)

SECTIONS OF CHAPTERS

(enabling subjects to be followed sequentially through all four chapters)

CHAPTER 1

Pre-School Years

1. Born into a colony
2. Meeting my immediate family
3. Connecting with friends beyond my immediate family
4. Attending an immigrant church
5. Getting acquainted with a neighborhood
6. Experiencing another Norwegian colony
7. Learning at home
8. Engaging in activities beyond home
9. Growing up: Beginning to identify my values
10. Evolving trust in my parents (and their trust in me)

CHAPTER 2

Grade School Years

1. Experiencing multiple colonies
2. Broadening my family
3. Finding additional friends
4. Beginning my spiritual journey
5. Playing outdoors in and beyond the colony

6. Deepening relationships in the second colony
7. Learning in grade school – Public School 169
8. Engaging in other activities beyond school
9. Growing up: Developing my values
10. Developing trust in others (and their trust in me)

CHAPTER 3

Junior High Years

1. Connecting with a peer colony
2. Finding an extended family
3. Cultivating relationships with friends
4. Deepening my spiritual journey
5. Becoming part of a particular neighborhood
6. Discovering increased freedom in the second colony
7. Learning in junior high school – Pershing 220
8. Engaging in activities beyond school
9. Growing up: Internalizing my values
10. Developing trust in myself

CHAPTER 4

Senior High Years

1. Belonging to a broader peer colony
2. Redefining connections within an extended family
3. Deepening relationships with friends
4. Expanding my spiritual journey
5. Interacting with multiple neighborhoods
6. Discovering other similar colonies
7. Learning in high school – Fort Hamilton 409
8. Engaging in activities beyond school
9. Growing up: Broadening my values
10. Developing trust in God (and God's trust in me)

READER'S REFLECTION

YOU'VE READ ABOUT THE FIRST 17 YEARS OF MY LIFE. NOW IT'S YOUR turn to think about how you might respond.

You might decide simply to reflect on what you've read—nothing more. Or, you might choose to develop some type of intentional way of responding. If it's the latter, you might consider carrying out one or more of the following possibilities:

- Beginning with yourself
- Spend some time thinking about your preschool years.
- Write notes of what comes to mind.
- Review what you've recorded—more than once.
- Ask yourself questions about what you've written.
- Write down your questions and the responses you've tentatively made.

1. Turning to others
    - Make a list of your friends during your first seventeen years.
    - Search for their contact information, particularly email addresses and phone numbers.
    - Get in touch with these friends, including contact

information for those on your list for whom you are lacking such information.
- Discern whether there are ways to get together in person, or by using an internet option such as Zoom.
- Keep taking notes of the information you gather, inviting ideas for additional resources for you to explore.

2. Organizing what you are learning.

3. Sharing what you are gathering, especially with your family and friends.

4. Discerning next steps in your ongoing reflection, perhaps writing your own memoir.

Have a good time doing whatever you decide!

RESOURCES

WEBSITES

americanscandinavian.org (American Scandinavian Society)

amscan.org (American Scandinavian Foundation)

brooklynhistory.org (Brooklyn Historical Society)

edvardgriegsociety.org (Edvard Grieg Society)

familyhistory@records.nyc.gov

heyridge.com (Bay Ridge News and Culture)

histreg.no (Historisk befolkningsregister)

info@norwayhouse.org

libertyellisfoundation.org/immigration-museum (Ellis Island National Museum of Immigration)

lifeinnorway.net (Life in Norway)

may17paradeny.com (Norwegian American 17th of May Committee)

naccusa.org (Norwegian American Chamber of Commerce)

naha@stolaf.edu (Norwegian-American Historical Association)

na-weekly.com (Norwegian American Weekly)

niahistory.org (Norwegian Immigration Association) - Includes Nordisk Tidende files.

noram.norway.com (Norwegian American Foundation)

nortrade.com (Norwegian Trade Council)

norway.com (Norwegian American Weekly)

norway.org (Consulate General of Norway NY)

norwegianamerican.com (The Norwegian Americans)

norwegianamerican.org (Norwegian Genealogical Association)

norwegiansworldwide.no (Nordmannsforbundet/Norwegians Worldwide)

scandinavian-museum.org (Scandinavian East Coast Museum)

scanfest.org (Scandinavian Fest)

sjomannskirken.no/newyork (Norwegian Seamen's Church NY)

sofn.com (Sons of Norway)

vesterheim.org (National Norwegian-American Museum & Heritage Center)

walterericksson.com (Walter Eriksson Virtual Museum)

FACEBOOK GROUPS

(listed by names they give themselves)

Bay Ridge Historical Society

Bay Ridge Talk

Born in Brooklyn

Brooklyn Born and Brooklyn Raised

Brooklyn Historical Society

Brooklyn History, Brooklyn Genealogy & Lost & Found

Brooklyn, New York Genealogy

Brooklyn Norwegians

Brooklyn Tales

Fort Hamilton High School Alumni

Friends Who Love Brooklyn, New York

Growing up in Brooklyn

Growing up in East New York, Brooklyn, 50's & 60's

Growing Up in Old Brooklyn, New York

I am a Brooklynite For Life! (Brooklyn NY)

I Grew Up in Brooklyn New York

Memories of Old Brooklyn NY

New York's Railroads, Subways & Trolleys Past & Present

Norden Hall: Northern European Culture, Customs, Cuisine & More!

Norway Weekly (from Life in Norway)

Norwegian-American Genealogical Association

Norwegian Day Parade of Brooklyn, New York

Norwegian Genealogy

Norwegian Holiday Traditions

Norwegian Immigration Association, Inc. (NIA)

Norwegian Seamen's Church

Official Sons of Norway Facebook Group

Remembering Brooklyn

Salem Gospel Tabernacle & Camp Challenge

Scandinavian ancestry (Av skandinavisk aett!)

Scandinavian Festivals

Sons of Norway

Southern Brooklyn Scrapbook

Staten Island NY in Days Gone By

The History of Brooklyn, New York

The One and Only Bay Ridge, Brooklyn

BOOKS AND ARTICLES

(selected by relevance to this volume)

Bjorkman, Stig. *Woody Allen on Woody Allen.* New York: Grove Press, 1993.

Della Femina, Jerry and Charles Sopkin. *An Italian Grows in Brooklyn.* Boston: Little, Brown and Company, 1978.

Frommer, Myrna Katz and Harvey Frommer. *It Happened in Brooklyn: An Oral History of Growing Up in the Borough in the 1940s, 1950s, and 1960s.* New York: Harcourt Brace & Company, 1993.

Hansen, Adolf. *Is It Time? Helping Laity and Clergy Discuss Homosexuality One Question at a Time.* Nashville: Abingdon Press, 2017.

__________, *Responding to Loss: A Resource for Caregivers.* New York: Baywood Publishing, 2004.

__________, *Three Simple Truths: Experiencing Them in Our Lives.* Portland, OR: Inkwater Press, 2014.

Hansen, Adolf, and Naomi Hansen. *Caring for Those Who Remain: A Practical Guide for End-of-Life Preparation.* Portland, OR: Inkwater Press, 2016.

Hansen, Adolf, with eight younger colleagues. *Becoming a Disciple: A Lifelong Venture.* Nashville: Abingdon Press, 2015.

Hassing, Arne. *Church Resistance to Nazism in Norway, 1940-1945 (New Directions in Scandinavian Studies).* Seattle: University of Washington Press, 2014. (Additional bibliographic entries in the Preface.)

Hess, Peg McCartt, Brenda McGowan, and Michael Botsko. *Nurturing the One, Supporting the Many: The Center for Family Life in Sunset Park, Brooklyn.* New York: Columbia University Press, 2003.

Jonassen, Christer. *The Norwegians in Bay Ridge: A Sociological Study of an Ethnic Group.* New York University: Dissertation, 1947.

Leddy, Kevin. *My Brooklyn . . . Your Brooklyn.* Bloomington, Indiana: Xlibris, 2017.

Lurie, April. *Dancing in the Streets of Brooklyn.* New York: Delacorte Press, 2002.

Mauk, David. *The Colony that Rose from the Sea: Norwegian Maritime and Community in Brooklyn, 1850-1910.* New York: Norwegian-American Historical Association, 1997.

McCullough, David. *Brooklyn . . . And How It Got That Way.* New York: Dial Press, 1983.

Meltzer, Maxwell. *A Boy Grows in Brooklyn.* Lulu Publishing, 2015.

Mybre, Liv Irene, ed. *Norwegians in New York: Builders of City, Community, and Culture.* NIA, Inc., 2000.

Nilsen, Lars. *Norway's Presence in New York City.* Norwegian Immigration Association (available from niahistory.org/the-history-of-norwegians-in-new-york/).

Pazmino, Robert. *A Boy Grows in Brooklyn: An Educational and Spiritual Memoir.* Eugene, Oregon: Wipf & Stock, 2014.

Ringdal, Siv. *Lapskaus Boulevard: Et Gjensyn med det norske Brooklyn.* Translated by Floyd Nilsen. Golden Slippers, 2012.

Robbins, Michael, editor. *Brooklyn: A State of Mind (125 Original Stories from America's Most Colorful City)*. New York: Workman Publishing, 2001.

Rubin, Cynthia Elyce. *Memories and Greetings from Norwegian America.* Seattle, Washington: The Norwegian American, 2021.

Rygg, Andreas Nilsen. *Norwegians in New York, 1825-1925.* New York: Norwegian News, 1941.

Semmingsen, Ingrid. *Norway to America: A History of the Migration.* Trans. By Einar Haugen. Minneapolis: University of Minnesota Press, 1978.

Simonsen, Jan Carol. *Brooklyn Girl: Growing Up Norwegian in New York City.* 2021.

Smith, Betty. *A Tree Grows in Brooklyn.* New York: HarperCollins Publishers, 1943.

Talese, Gay. *The Bridge: The Building of the Verrazzano-Narrows Bridge.* New York: Harper and Row, 1964.

Terdal, Leif. *Our Escape from Nazi-Occupied Norway: Norwegian Resistance to Nazism.* Trofford Publishing, 2008.

Vallier, Kevin and Michael Weber, eds. *Social Trust: Foundational and Philosophical Issues.* London: Routledge, 2021.

Wakefield, Dan. *New York in the Fifties.* New York: St. Martin's Press, 1992.

Wikipedia – *Bay Ridge, Brooklyn.* Last edited January 31, 2021.

Wikipedia – *Levittown, Hempstead, Long Island.* Last edited June 2, 2015.

Wikipedia – *Sunset Park, Brooklyn.* Last edited July 28, 2017.

Willensky, Elliot. *When Brooklyn Was the World: 1920-1957.* New York: Harmony Books, 1986.

Made in United States
North Haven, CT
01 July 2022